Do It Yourself
Online Reputation Management

*A Step-By-Step Guide For Building
Or Repairing Your Online Reputation*

By Herbert Tabin and Craig Agranoff

Copyright @ 2010 Herbert Tabin and Craig Agranoff
Published By Pendant Publishing — www.pendantpublishing.net
Copy Editor: John William Johnson
Book Designer and Compositor: Rosamond Grupp
ISBN: 978-0-578-05086-7
Printing History– First Edition: March, 2010

While every precaution has been taken in preparing this book, the publisher and author assume no responsibility for errors and omissions, or for damages resulting from the use of the information contained herein. Technology and services are constantly changing and therefore might contain errors and/or information that, while accurate when it was written, may be no longer accurate by the time you read it. Your use of or reliance on the information in this book is at your own risk and the author and Pendant Publishing disclaim and responsibility for any resulting damage or expense. The content of this book represents the views of the authors only, and does not represent the views of Pendant Publishing.

Notice of Rights – All rights reserved. No part of this book may be reproduced or transmitted in any form by any means, electronic, mechanical, photocopying, recording, or otherwise, without the prior written permission of the publisher. For information on getting permission for reprints and excerpts, contact info@pendantpublishing.net.

Notice of Liability – The information in this book is distributed on an "As Is" basis without warranty. While every precaution has been taken in the preparation of the book, neither the author nor Pendant Publishing shall have any liability to any person or entity with respect to any loss or damage caused or alleged to be caused directly or indirectly by the instructions contained in this book or by the computer software and hardware products described in it.

Trademarks – Many of the designations used by manufacturers and sellers to distinguish their products are claimed as trademarks. Where those designations appear in this book, and Pendant Publishing was aware of a trademark claim, the designations appear as requested by the owner of the trademark. All other product names and services identified throughout this book are used in editorial fashion only and for the benefit of such companies with no intention of infringement of the trademark. No such use, or the use of any trade name, is intended to convey endorsement or other affiliation with this book.

Foreword

*It takes 20 years to build a reputation
and five minutes to destroy it.
— Warren Buffett*

Maybe this is your story. Your life was going along just fine and then suddenly is thrown into turmoil by a blogger or a group of people maliciously posting online views about you. Now whenever someone Google's™ your name the search results show you have become the latest victim of online smear.

Acting solely as judge, jury and executioner, these anonymous people have purposefully altered your online persona. Worst of all, it cost them absolutely nothing but time to do so. Now the fruits of that malicious labor are ruining your life as people actually believe what's displayed online about you. Is there anything you can do?

The answer is YES! Just as bad information can be added to the Internet, good information can be added as well. In some instances you also may be able to have the bad information removed altogether. Much of what you need to fight for and preserve your online reputation is right here within these pages.

In purchasing this book you have taken the first step to win the reputation recovery battle. It will take some time and diligence but be comforted in the fact that you are not alone. Today everyone is susceptible to online ruin. The following chapters show you how to help yourself recover.

About The Authors

Herbert Tabin is a consultant, entrepreneur, venture capitalist, merger and acquisition expert as well as a noted specialist in online reputation management and monitoring. He has worked with many Internet startups and founded Vois.com, the blog sCommerce.com and operated Rev2.org. Herb Tabin has been featured on the cover of Entrepreneur Magazine - Entrepreneurs Business Start-Ups, The Palm Beach Post, and in Steve Spalding's book – 'All the Little Things' – Get the advice you will need to get your idea out of the garage and onto the web. He is a frequent speaker at techology events such as Refresh and LaidOffCamp.

Over the years he has received various entrepreneurial award nominations including Ernst and Young's Entrepreneur of the Year Award, received The Award for Business Leadership. He was also nominated as a finalist for best Large Scale Social Network, winning best "Photo Sharing Website Category" at Mashable's™ Open Web Awards. In March 2000, the State University of New York At Oneonta named its largest computer lab, the 'Tabin Computer Lab'.

Craig Agranoff is an entrepreneur, and national Social Media consultant as well as a noted specialist in online reputation management and monitoring. He has worked with many Internet startups and founded the tech blog sCommerce.com and edits Rev2.org. He also is a Tech/Social Media Correspondent in the New Times, VentureBeat.com, and Reviews.Vois.

Agranoff has been featured in the Miami Herald, New Times, The Palm Beach Post, AOL Digital Cities, Slice, CenterNetworks, Thrillist and The Sun-Sentinel. Also has appeared on Gary Vaynerchuck's Wine Library TV, Fox News, and CBS News.

He is a frequent speaker at tech events such as Refresh, New Tech Community, Bar Camp and LaidOffCamp. He was also nominated at Mashable's Open Web Awards as a finalist for best Large Scale Social Network, winning best "Photo Sharing Website Category".

Additionally, in his spare time, Craig's the Pizza Expert and founder of WorstPizza.com.

Table Of Contents

Chapter 1 — Understanding Your Online Reputation — 1

- What Is Your Online Reputation? 1
- How Did That Get On There? 2
- Can I Really Fix It Myself? 4
- What is Online Reputation Management? 5
- How Do Search Engines Work? 7
- How Long Will It Take? 9
- Why Legal Action May Not Work 11
- Why Some Search Engines Are More Important 12

Chapter 2 — Like It Or Not – You Are Being "Googled™" — 15

- Check "You" Out 15
- You No Longer Own Your Reputation 17

- Deep Research 17
- Other Deep Search Resources 24
- The Ultimate Deep Search 25
- Right To Your Phone 28
- Tools To Stay Informed About Changes 31
- More Alert Tools 40

Chapter 3 — The Importance of Personal Branding   41

- Your "Online" Reputation is Everything 41
- Personal Branding 42
- How Social Media Is Altering the Internet 45

Chapter 4 — Getting Started - Fixing The Problem   47

- Build Walls 47
- Dilution Is The Solution to Pollution 48

Chapter 5 — Using Social Profiles — 51

- Profile Building 51
- Rules of Profile Building 53
- Create A Central Email Account 55
- The Fantastic Five – The Fast Track 56
- The Terrific Twenty – Join These Too 69
- More Websites You Should Join 89

Chapter 6 — Using Photo Sharing Websites to Fix Your Reputation — 97

- Adding Pictures Can Improve Your Reputation 97

Chapter 7 — Using Video Sharing Websites To Fix Your Reputation — 101

- How Posting Videos Can Improve Your Reputation 101

Chapter 8 — Domain Names and Websites   107

- Do You Own Your Own Name? 107
- I Own My Own Name. Now What? 112
- Google "Insurance"? 116

Chapter 9 — Blogs – Your Internet Diary   119

- What is a Blog? 119

Chapter 10 — Guest Blogging   125

- What is Guest Blogging? 125
- Quick Tips 126

Chapter 11 — Being a Community Member Helps   129

- Just Ask 129

Chapter 12 — Using Pay-Per-Post Blogs Sites   133

- Paid Bloggers Can Quickly Help 133

Chapter 13 — How To Use Press Releases in ORM   139

- Your Friend – The Media 139
- Using Press Releases 139
- What is a Press Release? 140
- How To Create a Press Release 140
- Free and Pay Press Release Services 143
- The Free Firms 146

Chapter 14 — How to Remove Search Engines Information   149

- Where to Begin – The Webmaster 149
- How to Contact a Webmaster 149
- Removing Information from Google 151
- Removing Information From Google 151

- Removing Information From Yahoo 155
- Removing Information From Blogger 159
- Removing Information At ZoomInfo 161

Chapter 15 — Online Reputation Management is Ongoing   167

- Today – Tomorrow – Forever 167

Chapter 1
Understanding Your Online Reputation

What is Your Online Reputation?

Your "Online Reputation" is two simple things:

- What the Internet says about you.
- The way you are perceived on the Internet by others.

When you do a Google search on your name, what comes up on the first results page? Is there anything on there that you'd rather not have anyone read? If so, it can become a major problem.

Today a majority of people research other people, using the Internet as the primary, or "default" destination for information on businesses and individuals.

More importantly, people believe what they read on Google. With this in mind, it is more important than ever to protect your online reputation.

How Did That Get On There?

How did you and your information get on the Internet in the first place?

There are many answers to that question. However, the majority of your Internet information got there in one of three ways.

- Gathered, or "aggregated" from public document filings or other public sources, including the news media.

- Put up there by you.

- Put there by a third party.

Now that it's up there, you want to know:

Can it be removed?

Can it be fixed?

The short answer is "yes". But most importantly is that you need to understand an important reality: "Hope is Not a Strategy." To repair or protect your online reputation you need to take action.

Just hoping that the bad things about you listed on search engines will go away quietly won't work. Remember that Google is a Machine. You taking control of your content means just that: Insuring that the newest and most accurate information that you want displayed is available online so that Internet searches find it rather than other information that you would rather not have be seen.

Any information you find was originally placed there by a human. Likewise, it will take another human, you, to take control of what is on the Internet about you. Ironically, what it really comes down to is that the more you put on the Internet about yourself, the more control you will have in what the Internet says about you!

Can I Really Fix It Myself?

You're skeptical. Maybe you're thinking "I don't understand the Internet at all and this will be too hard for me to do on my own".

While it is true that today's Internet is full of scary sounding "buzzwords" what it takes to control your online reputation isn't as complicated as you might think. All it takes is a few minutes a day following the simple steps contained within this book.

Remember "Hope Is Not a Strategy". This book is arranged specifically so that you see results almost immediately. Once you see results, you will then see the value of maintaining your name and reputation on the Internet.

What is Online Reputation Management?

The process of controlling your online reputation is known as Online Reputation Management (ORM). ORM works by suppressing negative information about you to the bottom of search engine results while driving positive information to the top.

Don't confuse Online Reputation Management with another common Internet term — Search Engine Optimization (SEO) or Search Engine Marketing (SEM).

Search Engine Optimization is the process whereby webmasters optimize websites for optimal search engine results while Search Engine Marketing is the use of various marketing techniques designed to increase search engine traffic.

ORM is completely different. Online Reputation Management is different in that the focus is to actually bring down current search results by replacing the top results with new results provided by your Online Reputation Management campaign.

To control your online reputation means owning it. The only way to own your online reputation is to become totally transparent. Simply, the more you put on the Internet the more you control your online destiny.

How Do Search Engines Work?

Search engines like Google, Yahoo and Bing are search tools designed to scour for information on the Internet — and to do so millions of times more quickly than any human being could.

When a user begins a query by entering keywords into a search engine box, the engine examines its index and provides "search results", listing the best-matching web pages according to its criteria.

The basic results are accompanied by a short summary containing the document's title and parts of the text. The index is built from the information stored with the data and the method by which the information is indexed.

Unlike Web directories, which are maintained by human editors, search engines operate algorithmically or are a mixture of algorithmic and human input. The usefulness of a search engine depends on the relevance of the "result set" it gives back.

While there may be millions of web pages including a word or phrase, some pages are more relevant, popular, or authoritative than others. Most search engines employ methods to create results which list the "best" pages first.

How a search engine decides which pages are the best — and the order the results should be shown — varies widely from one engine to another. The methods also change over time as Internet usage changes and new techniques evolve.

Search engines work by Web Crawling, Indexing and Searching. Web search engines work by storing information about many web pages, which they retrieve from the HTML (*Hyper Text Markup Language,* the predominant markup language for web pages) itself. These pages are retrieved by a Web crawler or "Spider" — an automated Web browser which follows every link on the site. The contents of each page are then analyzed to determine how each should be indexed. Words may also be extracted from the titles, headings, or special fields called "meta tags".

Data about web pages is then stored in an index database for use in later queries.

The purpose of an index is to allow information to be found quickly. Like many search engines, Google stores all or part of the source page referred to as a "cache", as well as information about the web pages. These cached pages always hold the actual search text since it is the one that was actually indexed. Increased search relevance makes these cached pages very useful, even beyond the fact that they may contain data that may no longer be available elsewhere.

How Long Will It Take?

The first question everyone asks about fixing an online reputation is how long is it going to take? The answer really depends on many different factors, such as the volume of content already online about you as well as how many negative items need to be suppressed.

Most of the time you can see new items that you have created online as quickly as 2-7 days and search engine content rearrangement in 4 to 5 weeks if properly executed. Overall results of a successful campaign will be seen within 8 to 12 weeks.

There are many reasons why it takes so long overall and the biggest is the search engines themselves. First is that any information you may add to the Internet takes time until it is indexed. Google for instance crawls or "spiders" new items on the Internet approximately every 3 or 4 days meaning that if you add something to the Internet it may be up to 4 days before that information is crawled.

After the information is crawled it then needs to be indexed according to its relevance. Search engines also work on algorithms designed to notice anomalies.

Google penalizes anyone for publishing content too quickly on its search engine and see this as an anomaly leading it to think the search engine is getting spammed. If Google thinks this, they will ignore the posts and will "Sandbox" those efforts.

Do not attempt to create 50 new items like web pages, Blog posts, articles, or links in a day or you will quickly discover it is a waste of time and will be ignored by the search engines. A simple rule of thumb, to make it appear as if content is naturally flowing onto the web, is to only add 1 or 2 items every 2 days. This should assure you of having a successful online reputation management campaign and not cause a negative impact. This is why results of a campaign can take several weeks.

Why Legal Action May Not Work

You're angry. You don't like what you see online about yourself and your first reaction is to pursue legal action. Unfortunately, legal action is often futile for two reasons:

- The Communication Decency Act of 1996, gives, a sort of, "virtual immunity" to Web sites themselves that host information posted online.

- The uniquely non-physical nature of the Web itself lends to a variety of legal quagmires including legal jurisdiction issues. That is assuming that even if you can actually find your defamer who could be hiding behind a series of fake email addresses and rolling IP addresses.

Why Some Search Engines Are More Important

"All animals are equal, but some animals are more equal than others," according to author George Orwell in his book *Animal Farm*.

While it's important to have a good reputation throughout the Internet there are some search engines that are more important. The fact is, as of the writing of this book, some 65.4 percent of all searches are conducted using Google and as such Google is the search engine that you should focus on most.[1]

---

[1] http://blog.nielsen.com/nielsenwire/online_mobile/top-u-s-online-search-providers-november-2009

Rank	Provider	Searches	Share
1	Google Search	6,546,172	65.4%
2	Yahoo! Search	1,525,964	15.3%
3	MSN/Windows Live/Bing Search	1,073,416	10.7%
4	AOL Search	280,311	2.8%
5	Ask.com Search	177,589	1.8%
6	My Web Search Search	101,586	1.0%
7	Comcast Search	47,746	0.5%
8	NexTag Search	34,314	0.3%
9	BizRate Search	29,044	0.3%
10	Yellow Pages Search	25,260	0.3%

Searches represent the total number of queries conducted at the provider. Example: An estimated 6.5 billion search queries were conducted at Google Search, representing 65.4 percent of all search queries conducted during the given time period.

Chapter 2
Like It Or Not – You Are Being "Googled"

Check "You" Out

"Google it" is now a household phrase.

You should assume that your prospective employer, any new business contact or prospective mates are researching you online. Whether you wan to believe it or not you have been Googled.

What you should be wondering about is what is found when you are Googled.

Try it. Do a vanity search on your name. What do you see? Do you have any pictures or videos of yourself online that are questionable? The power of the Internet begins with its speed. Because of that speed, we can become our own worst enemy if not careful, i.e., is there a blog you wrote or responded to in a moment of anger that you regret?

Beyond that, and because of easy and quick access to the Internet, you need to spend time and thought about developing your own personal brand — a positive brand, because all kinds of people are doing searches on you. As a professional, what you want to accomplish with your image is credibility. You want those search results to show that you know what you're doing and that you have integrity.

It is difficult to thrive in today's Internet connected world without having control of your image, or personal brand.

The fact is, if you have an online presence — even a slight one -- people are making assumptions and forming opinions about you. You're being placed into categories and conclusions drawn each and every day. Whether you like it or not, each of the categories and conclusions, constitute your image.

Now add to this Internet stew the following: if you are not controlling your personal brand, someone else potentially can. This is one of the primary reasons you need to develop and control your personal Internet brand.

You No Longer Own Your Reputation

Do you know all everything that is on the Internet about you? Probably not, because there's actually a lot more available out on the Internet than you may think. There's also the Deep Web — also called DeepNet

Deep Research

The Deep Web refers to WWW content that is not part of the surface Web which is indexed by standard search engines. In fact, most of the Web's information is buried far down on dynamically generated sites, in online databases that general-purpose web crawlers cannot reach.

Traditional search engines like Google cannot "see" or retrieve content in the deep Web. The Deep Web is several orders of magnitude larger than the surface Web. Since most personal profiles, public records and other people-related documents are stored in databases and not on static web pages, most of the higher-quality information about people is simply "invisible" to a regular search engine.

Earlier in this chapter we suggested a "vanity search" whereby you could see what basic information comes up when people search for you on Google or Yahoo. But what if you knew where to dig deeper to find out information about yourself online?

Let's try a "vanity search" again — but with deep search engines that search the deep web for free and be prepared to be amazed. The four main free web deep resource websites are:

- Whoozy
- PIPL
- Yasni
- PeekYou

Whoozy — http://whoozy.com

Whoozy is a search engine about people. It searches the web for information about a particular person and uses search engines, social networks and picture/video/audio sites to gather relevant info.

When you type in a name, Whoozy software does an intense search, resulting in a straightforward interface enabling you to quickly see the available information about you or whoever is searched.

To protect yourself on Whoozy you can register with the site. Whoozy then gives you the ability to add desirable search results to your profile by creating a personal profile and adding comments to search results for clarification.

Want to register? Go here: http://whoozy.com/register

Yasni — http://www.yasni.com

Yasni is the world's most popular people search engine. More than 10 million people worldwide visit Yasni each month. More and more people turn to Yasni to find information about old friends.

Yasni puts an end to multiple web searches. Find everything about yourself, friends, neighbors or business partners. It allows you to be the first to know when something new is published about you on the web with weekly email updates.

Within seconds, Yasni provides a comprehensive overview of a person, including associated networks, contacts, pictures and other publicly available information.

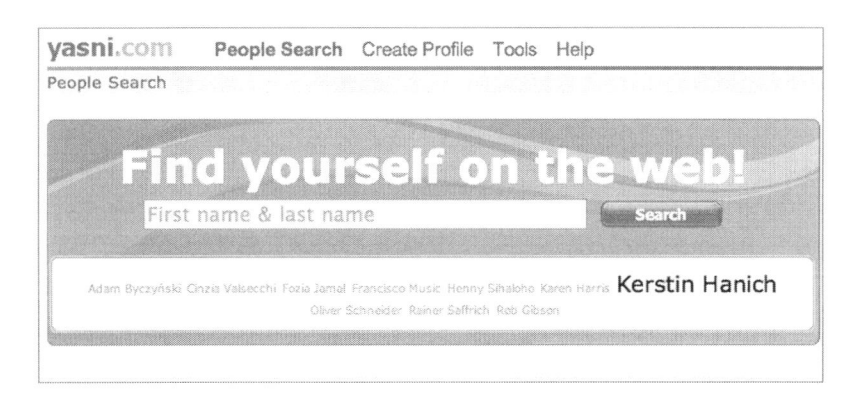

Better still, Yasni is also the ultimate resource to control one's online reputation and manage what Web information is available about you. This includes differentiating yourself from persons with the same name, but perhaps a less than desirable reputation.

Yasni allows you to control the content associated with your name and helps protect your reputation. It only takes a few clicks to create a Yasni profile and your Yasni profile will be found on major search engines such as Google or Yahoo.

Want to create a Yasni profile?
Go here: http://www.yasni.com/index.php?action=webprofile&nameblank=1&wnsb

PIPL — http://pipl.com

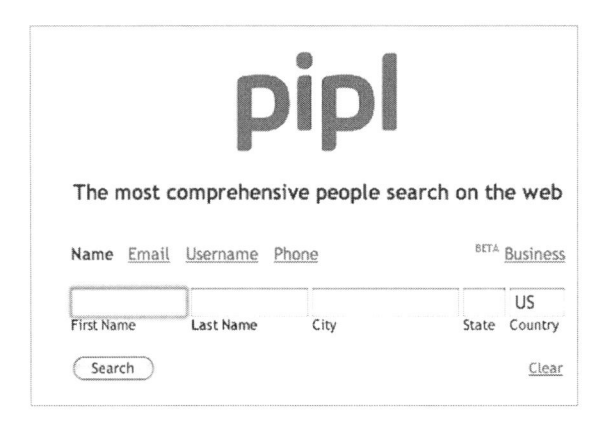

Pipl's query-engine also helps you find deep web pages that cannot be found on regular search engines. Pipl robots are set to interact with searchable databases and extract facts, contact details and other relevant information from personal profiles, member directories, scientific publications, court records and numerous other deep-web sources.

Pipl is not just about finding more results. Pipl uses advanced language-analysis and ranking algorithms to bring you the most relevant bits of information about a person in a single, easy-to-read results page.

PeekYou — http://www.peekyou.com

A PeekYou profile helps other people find your websites, social-networking pages, photos or anything else about you online.

You can also register to become a full "contributor" which allows you to track your edits to PeekYou and gives you other benefits as well.

Want to register? Go here: http://www.peekyou.com/register/index.php

Other Deep Search Resources

- Spokeo.com
- Wink.com
- Rapleaf.com
- Zabasearch.com
- iSearch.com
- 123people.com
- Whoisi.com
- Spock.com
- WhoIsHim.com

Some of these deep search websites allow you to register. If you find conflicting information on any of these sites, register and take control of each profile that has been formed.

The Ultimate Deep Search

The ultimate deep search requires you to dig — that is, dig in your wallet and pay for deep search tools and services.

While the Internet provides a lot of information for free, private databases exist that can offer much more information, i.e., Intelius and Intelius Mobile are the ultimate in background checks.

These pay-for-services cannot be altered like the Internet, but when you need the best source of information, there's nothing better.

Intelius — http://www.intelius.com

Intelius is an online public records company, offering a variety of services to both consumers and businesses including civil and criminal records. Known primarily for its background search service, Intelius is at the forefront of providing background searches for dating, specifically online dating.

INTELIUS
Live in the know.™

Sign In – My Intelius
View My Reports

Verification Services
- Background Check
- Reverse Phone Lookup
- Property & Neighborhood

Information Services
- ▸ People Search
- Email Search
- Social Net Search

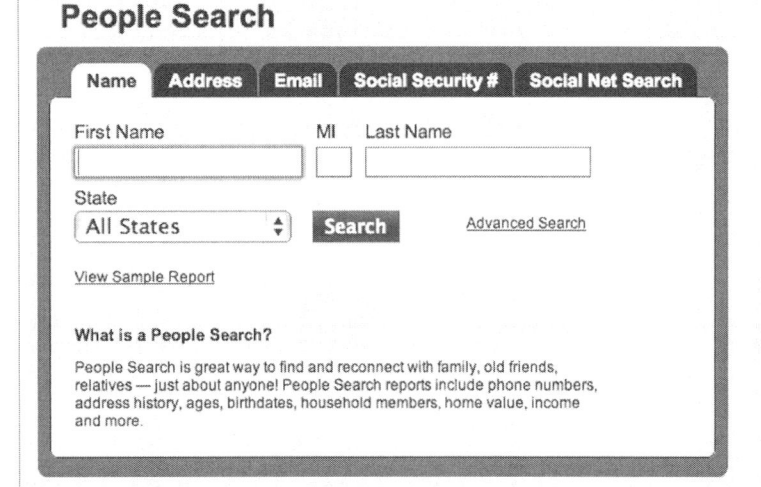

Protection Services
- Reverse Cell Phone Directory
- Identity Protect
- Criminal & Sex Offender

Business Services
- Employee Screening
- Tenant Screening
- All Products & Services

NEW — SELF CHECK DRIVING RECORD REPORT - Instant! [SEARCH NOW ▸] *"Find Out What's On Your Driving Record"*

People Search

| **Name** | Address | Email | Social Security # | Social Net Search |

First Name   MI   Last Name

State: All States   [Search]   Advanced Search

View Sample Report

What is a People Search?

People Search is great way to find and reconnect with family, old friends, relatives — just about anyone! People Search reports include phone numbers, address history, ages, birthdates, household members, home value, income and more.

Reverse Phone Lookup

| **Phone** |

Phone Number: (ex. 555-555-5555)   [Search]

View Sample Report

What is a Reverse Phone Lookup?

Know who is calling you or your family! The report includes name, phone owner details, and more for any cell phone, unlisted, non-published, or other phone numbers.

For $39.95, Intelius will do a background search of public records and provide information on virtually anyone. In addition to background checks for dating, Intelius markets its services to landlords, employers, and other businesses.

By also providing credit checks, criminal and sex offender checks, and reverse phone directory services, Intelius utilizes its valuable database to provide many types of information — at a price.

However, Intelius also has some free services: "People Search" and "Email Search". Also you can obtain limited information by entering a social security number, cellular phone number, or address.

Right To Your Phone

Intelius Mobile — http://www.intelius.com/mobile

Intelius mobile is a free mobile app that deciphers fact from fiction in the palm of your hand. Simply enter a name, phone number or email address and instantly get accurate and comprehensive results.

The new iPhone app called Share Date Check also allows you to run a criminal background check on your mobile phone. Once it's downloaded on an iPhone, the application only needs a name or cell phone number to search publicly available records. Date Check is available for download in Apple's App store and will be available soon in Android and BlackBerry versions

If you activate the app's "Sleaze Detector", it scans criminal records to determine if anyone with that name has been charged with drug possession, assault and battery, sex crimes, DUI and other offenses.

If you click Net Worth, it looks for information about home ownership and property value. It can also check social networking sites, such as LinkedIn to provide employment and education information.

Be aware that though the app itself is free, the services can cost up to $40 per search, depending on the kind of searches that are selected.

Learn about it here: http://www.youtube.com/watch?v=N5PgprRbQLs

Tools To Stay Informed About Changes

One of the most important things about managing your online reputation is monitoring. You should constantly monitor what is being said about you online using online alerts and feeds to catch every mention of your name, brand, domain, etc.

The primary reason you need to stay informed is you so you can take action immediately after discovering any problematic information added to the internet, before, that information escalates or enters the top search results. Basically, you can't attack something if you don't know its there. With monitoring tools you are virtually first to see the problem. There are many types of tools that can help you manage your online reputation, but the following are the most comprehensive and user-friendly solutions.

Google Alerts – www.google.com/alerts

To quickly monitor your reputation on Google, perform a vanity search on Google and then click right below the Google Search Box on the button that says Show Options. Click the button and you will see a side bar open that has a series of options for All results and Any time. By clicking the buttons under Any Time you can see latest results on you for the past 24 hours, past week or past year.

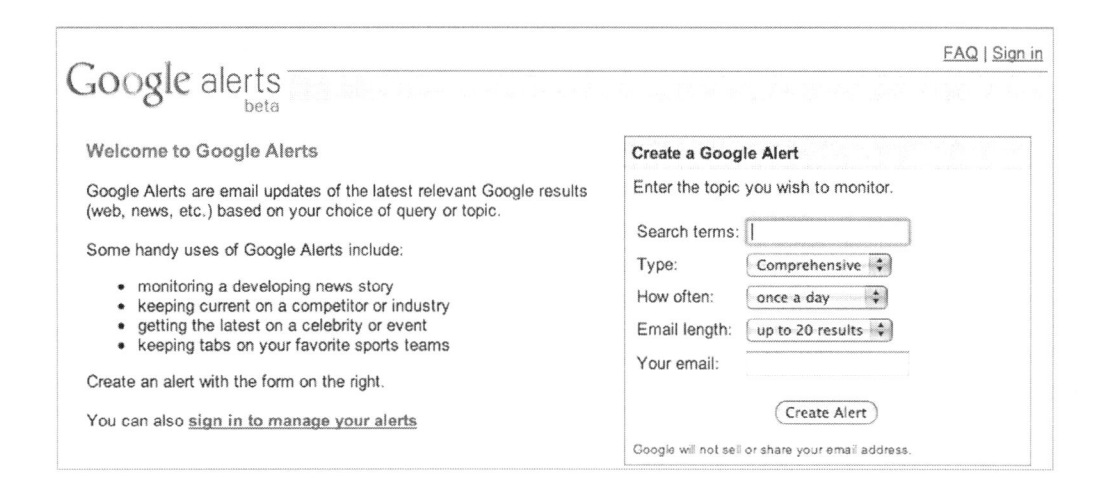

Google Alerts is a service which notifies its users by email, or as a feed, about user preferred web and news pages. Google currently offers several types of alert searches: "News", "Web", "Blogs", "Comprehensive", "Video" and "Groups".

- A news alert is an email that lets the user know if new articles make it into the top ten results of his/her Google News search.

- A web alert is an email that lets the user know if new web pages appear in the top twenty results for his/her Google Web search.

- A News and Web alert is an email that lets the user know when new articles related to his/her search term make it into the top ten results for a Google News search or the top 20 results for a Google Web search.

- A Groups alert is an email that lets the user know if new posts make it into the top fifty results of his/her Google Groups search.

Google Alerts also allow its users to determine the frequency in which checks are made for new results. Three options are available: "once a day", "once a week", or "as it happens".

These options do not necessarily control how often you will receive alerts. The first option, for example, means you would receive at most one alert email per day. The "as it happens" option can result in many alert emails per day, depending on the search. Google Alerts are available in plain text, as well as HTML.

Windows Live Alerts — http://alerts.live.com

Windows Live Alerts, formerly MSN Alerts, allows users to get notification of time-sensitive events and information from various alert content providers. Users are able to choose how and when to receive alerts. Windows Live Alerts is a free service for users with a Windows Live ID. Alerts to wireless devices are available in the United States, Canada and China only.

Yahoo Alerts — http://alerts.yahoo.com

Yahoo! Alerts is a free, personalized notification service that instantly informs you about what you consider important and relevant via email, instant message, pager, or cell phone. You can sign in (or sign up to get a Yahoo! account) and customize your Yahoo! Alerts content and how it is delivered. Yahoo! offers free alerts on the following content:

- Avatars Alerts: Get updates on new clothes, backgrounds, gear, and more on Yahoo! Avatars.

- Breaking News Alerts: Receive news as soon as it happens

- Missing Children incidents reported in your chosen region.

- News Alerts: Customize your news using our powerful keyword news search tools and receive summaries of top stories in various categories.

And to modify your Yahoo! alerts at anytime, go here: http://alerts.yahoo.com/myalerts.php

Google Reader — www.google.com/reader

Google Reader constantly checks your favorite news sites and blogs for new content and as such any mention of any information you might want to monitor such as your name or information on your reputation. Use Google Reader's built-in public page to easily share interesting items with your friends and family.

Google Reader is totally free and works in most modern browsers, without any software to install. Google Reader shows you all of your favorite sites in one convenient place. It's like a personalized inbox for the entire web. Millions of sites publish feeds with the latest updates; Google Reader feed search makes it easy to find new content that interests you.

Want to check it out? http://www.google.com/intl/en/googlereader/tour.html

Twitter Search — http://search.twitter.com

Twitter's search feature enables you to find mentions of your company, brand, or products in almost real-time, enabling you to take swift and immediate action if necessary.

Keeping up with interesting news and people you care about is one dimension of Twitter. But what if you need to find out what's happening in the world beyond your personal timeline? There is an undeniable need to search, filter, and otherwise interact with the volumes of news and information being transmitted to Twitter every second.

Twitter Search helps you filter all the real-time information coursing through the service. Craft your queries using the many advanced search operators. You can also use the advanced search page to easily incorporate search operators in your queries.

Search Operators

You can type these search operators directly into the search box. (Alternatively, you can use the advanced search form to automatically constuct your query.)

Operator	Finds tweets...
twitter search	containing both "twitter" and "search". This is the default operator.
"happy hour"	containing the exact phrase "happy hour".
love **OR** hate	containing either "love" or "hate" (or both).
beer -root	containing "beer" but not "root".
#haiku	containing the hashtag "haiku".
from:alexiskold	sent from person "alexiskold".
to:techcrunch	sent to person "techcrunch".
@mashable	referencing person "mashable".
"happy hour" **near**:"san francisco"	containing the exact phrase "happy hour" and sent near "san francisco".
near:NYC **within**:15mi	sent within 15 miles of "NYC".
superhero **since**:2010-02-12	containing "superhero" and sent since date "2010-02-12" (year-month-day).
ftw **until**:2010-02-12	containing "ftw" and sent up to date "2010-02-12".
movie -scary :)	containing "movie", but not "scary", and with a positive attitude.
flight :(	containing "flight" and with a negative attitude.
traffic ?	containing "traffic" and asking a question.
hilarious **filter:links**	containing "hilarious" and linking to URLs.
news **source:twitterfeed**	containing "news" and entered via TwitterFeed

Twitter Home · About Twitter Search · API · Install Search Plugin

© 2010 Twitter, Inc.

twitter [Q Enter your query] (Search) Advanced Search

Advanced Search

Use this form to automatically construct your query. (Alternatively, you can type search operators directly into the search box.)

Find tweets based on... (Search)

Words
- All of these words
- This exact phrase
- Any of these words
- None of these words
- This hashtag
- Written in [Any Language] (persistent)

People
- From this person
- To this person
- Referencing this person

Places
- Near this place
- Within this distance [15] ● miles ○ kilometers

Dates
- Since this date
- Until this date

Attitudes
- With positive attitude :) ☐
- With negative attitude :(☐
- Asking a question ? ☐

Other
- Containing links ☐
- Include retweets ☐
- Results per page [15] (persistent)

(Search)

More Alert Tools

More alert tools to try include;

- Alerts.com
- Changedetection.com
- Knowem.com
- Monitorthis.com
- Notify.me
- Pingie.com
- Pressflip.com
- Swartmii.com
- Trackengine.com
- Trendrr.com
- Updatescanner.com
- Versionista.com
- Watchthatpage.com
- Whostalkin.com
- Wink.com
- Yotify.com
- Zabasearch.com

Chapter 3
The Importance of Personal Branding

Your "Online" Reputation is Everything

You've worked to establish a good name, integrity and a hard work ethic — in short, a good reputation.

Despite this, however, hostile entities out there can and will tarnish that reputation — and in our Internet world, online reputation is everything.

People believe what shows up on Google. Now is the time to take control of your image and your online legacy beginning with your personal brand.

Personal Branding

That's right — you're a brand, just like Coke, Pepsi, or McDonalds. Actually your personal brand is much more important than Coke, Pepsi, or McDonalds because your brand represents and financially supports you.

You are in fact the Chief Executive Office (CEO) of that brand called "You." And like most small firms, that also makes you chief marketer.

It's just that simple — and it doesn't have to be that hard, if you manage to use the Web, rather than allowing yourself to be used by the Web.

That's right. Whether you want to believe it or not, we are all now individual CEOs of that brand called "you, and the number one job at Brand You is to be head marketer.

The good news is that today with the Web everyone has an opportunity to stand out. That means, beginning today, you need to think of yourself differently; going forward you need to think of yourself as a brand.

So who are you?

To start, you need to develop a standard paragraph about yourself — something often called a "boilerplate." The boilerplate you develop will be used by you over and over again.

What should your boilerplate say?

Ask yourself: what is it about me, my product or service that makes me different? Start by identifying the qualities or characteristics that make you distinctive from your competitors or colleagues. What makes you stand out? What would your colleagues or customers say:

- Is your greatest strength?
- Your most noteworthy trait?
- Your best quality?

For instance - do you deliver your work on time? Do you solve problems before there's a crisis?

Forget your job title. Ask yourself: what do I do that adds distinctive value?

Forget your job description. Ask yourself: what do I do that I am most proud of? Ask yourself: what have I accomplished I can brag about? As a brand, you have to become focused on what you do that adds value, and for which you can take credit. And when you've done that, sit down and ask yourself one more question: What do I want to be known for?

Finally, and after going through this exercise, give yourself a 30-second "elevator pitch" challenge. Take the time to write down your answer and read it several times. If your answer doesn't grab you, then you have a problem. Your answer should light up the eyes of a prospective client or command a vote of confidence in your personal circle. It's time to give some serious thought and even more serious effort to imagining and developing yourself as a brand.

Still confused?

Let's look at the profile of Felicia Day. Felicia Day is most likely no one that you are particularly familiar with. Felicia is an aspiring actress who thoroughly understands the importance of developing her own brand. To get an idea of what good branding looks like we can look at her profile here:
http://en.wikipedia.org/wiki/Felicia_Day

How Social Media Is Altering The Internet

Social media is the new face of the Web. Just as the Internet revolutionized information sharing during the 1990s, today social media is radically altering how people communicate and share information.

To take control of your online reputation a solid social network presence is absolutely essential. Search engines like Google specifically recognize the power of social media, opting to include updates from Twitter, FriendFeed, Tumblr and other social sites in search results. Optimizing your online reputation with social media is becoming a must to gain top search position ranking.

Chapter 4
Getting Started - Fixing The Problem

The only real defense is active defense
— Mao Zedong

Build Walls

Forging your own online legacy before someone else does is paramount. Today you don't own your online reputation. Your reputation is created as an aggregation of content, and then indexed by a search engine.

What appears when your name is searched depends on what is on the Internet about you and if you do nothing to place content on the Internet about yourself — count on it, someone else will.

Often the content that others place on the Internet about you may not please you. That's why it's essential to build a wall of positive content. This works because if and when negative content is posted it will have a much harder time rising to the top of search results.

In short, you need to take positive action to publicize your own positive news, awards, school honors, etc. Doing so, can pre-empt the negative.

Dilution Is The Solution to Pollution

"Dilution is the solution to pollution," is a dictum which summarizes a traditional approach to pollution management whereby sufficiently diluted pollution is not harmful. The same idea directly applies to your online reputation. If you have a polluted reputation online you need to dilute that pollution.

You can do that by adding content to the Internet about you that not only dilutes the negative information, but will appear at the top of search engine results — pushing down negative results, diluting the negativity. To do this you can use the following ten techniques:

- Profile Building
- Photo Sharing
- Video Sharing
- Domain Name Use
- Blog Posting
- Guest Blogging
- Community Membership
- Paid Bloggers
- Press Releases
- Blog Post Removal Techniques

Chapter 5
Using Social Profiles

Besides being a great way to reach out to friends and customers, social profiles are becoming known for ranking high in Internet searches because of all the links pointed at them.

If you're looking to claim and make more positive your space on the Internet, creating Social Profile accounts is one of the best ways to go.

Profile Building

While there are many ways to change your online reputation, profile building will work a large percentage of the time. The overall goal is to have search engines display the information which you want seen. To do this you need to secure the first several pages of a Google, Yahoo and Bing search when your name is searched.

Securing the first pages makes it more difficult for something new to enter those pages — and even if it does it will soon be indexed in a lower position on a page that is deeper within the search results.

Keep in mind that most people do not go beyond the first page of search results. Profile building is an easy task that carries a lot of weight with search engines — and it's as simple as building a profile on various sites.

In short, if you have a lot of profiles online all those profiles will each be indexed under your name. While we're not recommending you create 200 profiles on every new website that emerges, we are suggesting that you create 25 profiles on the sites suggested below.

Doing so will quickly change the landscape of your search results. Do not create all 25 profiles in one day as Google and the other search engines will regard your effort as spam as previously discussed. The best approach is to create one profile a day for a month. You will see changes in your search results in just days.

All profiles and profile names should be the exact term/phrase that you desire ranking for.

Rules of Profile Building

Establish a profile on each site suggested, using the exact — and we mean, exact — profile name with which you desire to achieve rank. In most cases that means using your legal name or the name people will search when looking for you.

Add a picture to your profile (also use common sense and use a good clear picture or head shot of yourself). Change the pictures for each profile when possible because the pictures will be the images picked up in search results under your name.

Remember — use your real name and create a personalized url link for each profile. A good rule of thumb is to look at others who have joined the website and look to see what those personalized URLs looks like.

Barack Obama http://www.linkedin.com/pub/dir/Barack/Obama/

Jack Welch http://twitter.com/jack_welch

Try to gather a few friends on each of these sites; obviously the more the better. It works best if you take an active role and participate. Each friend will result in an internal link back to your profile on that site, making it stronger.

Within each site, try to secure links from the strongest profiles first — those hold the most weight. Also join groups where possible. Often these will pass link power to your profile as well. When possible, link to your other social profiles.

Create A Central Email Account

Before you begin creating profiles, create a new email account somewhere that will be used just for your alerts. It will also be used as the email address for the profiles you create.

You will need to create such an email account because each profile has the potential to generate a lot of email and this is not something you would want to add to your daily use email account.

Additionally this email account can be used to store the passwords created for your new profiles.

The Fantastic Five – The Fast Track

These are the five most important profiles you need to create and which almost always appear on top of search engines, or Page One.

- Google Profile
- Facebook
- LinkedIn
- Twitter
- ZoomInfo

Changing the way search engines view you can take up to six months in some cases to see results. That seems like an eternity — right?

Understanding that we live in a society where "instant gratification" is expected, the sites noted above are in the order of which rank high on most search results.

These same sites can put you on the fast track when starting your campaign to immediately improve your online presence, show you results quickly.

Google Profile

- **Website Link – www.google.com/profiles/me**

Who They Are And What They Do – Google advertises Google Profile with ads that say: "Control what people see when they search for you on Google!" You can thus control how you appear in Google by creating a personal profile that people will then see when doing web searches for your name. According to Google, a Google profile is simply how you present yourself on Google's line of products to other Google users. It allows you to control how you appear on Google and tells others a bit more about who you are.

Your Google Profile is guaranteed by Google to be on the bottom of Page 1 of your Google search results usually within a day of pushing the button.

Google Create your profile

What do people see when they find you online? You can control how you appear in Google by creating a personal profile...

Create my profile

Already have one?
Sign in to see your profile

Help people find the right information
when they search for you on Google.

Create a personal page
that links to your blog and other profiles.

Keep family and friends up to date
with your contact info and photos.

Learn more

...and people will see it on their results page when they do web searches for your name.

Check out some example profiles

Felicia Day	Elizabeth Jardina
Peter Cramton	M. Flourish Klink
Matt Cutts	Aileen Lee
Rachel Hansson	Tim O'Reilly
Jeff Huber	David Meerman Scott

©2010 Google - Google Home - Terms of Service - Privacy Policy - Help

You can include, for example, links to your blog, online photos, and other profiles such as Facebook, LinkedIn, and more. You have control over what others see. Your profile won't display any private information unless you've explicitly added it.

What we suggest you do is use your Google Profile as a way of cataloguing all the social profiles you create by adding those links to your Google Profile. Think about it like telling Google to go search for the links and add them to their search engine. This list you create will allow you to remember what Social websites you joined and created a profile on.

And the following list will guide you in setting up your Google profile.

- Receive messages. Enable the 'Send a message' feature to allow anyone with a Google Account to email you without revealing your email address.

- Add photos. Enhance your profile by adding photos from Flickr or Picasa.

- Create a page about you. Write a short bio in the About me tab

- Add your contact information. Share your information with your friends and family, so they always have the most up-to-date information. You control who sees it.

- Add links to your other profiles and sites. Create a record of your other content on the Web. You can link to Google content, including your Blogger blog, public Picasa Web Albums and Google Reader shared items as well as other pages on the Web such as Twitter, MySpace, Facebook, and LinkedIn.

- Show your location. 'My places' includes all the cities you've entered on your profile. Your current location and where you've lived are displayed on a map.

Another reason we suggest starting with Google Profile is because Google Profile has a feature which allows access to many of the sites recommended in this book to be joined with just a few keystrokes — cutting down time it takes to become a member of other sites.

Facebook.com

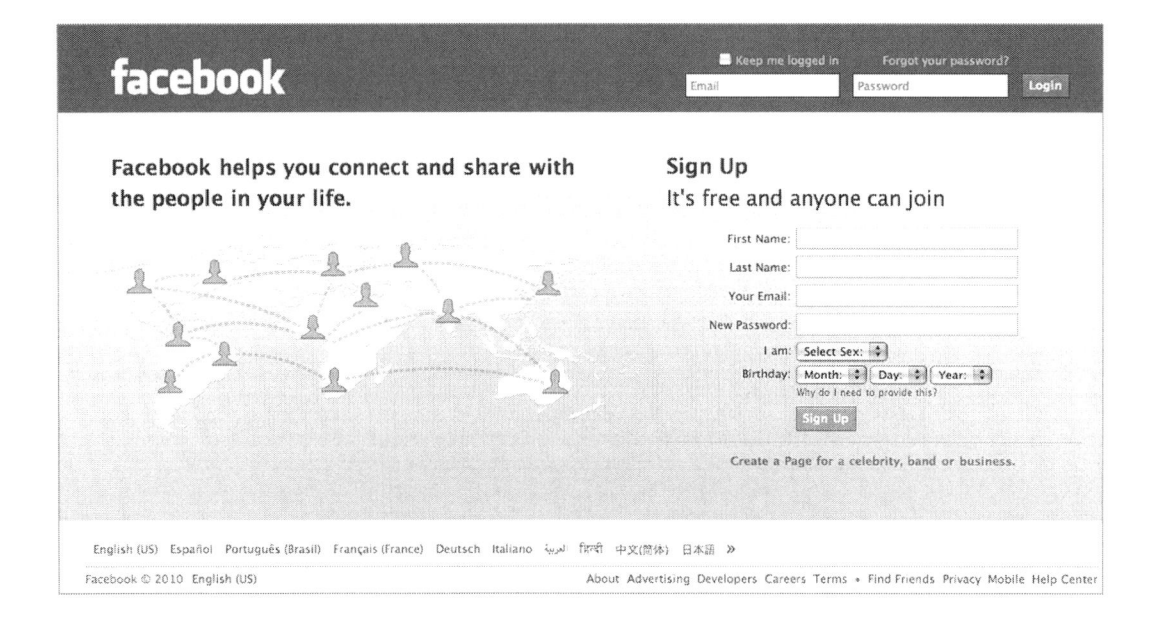

- **Website Link –** www.facebook.com
- **Join Link –** http://www.facebook.com/r.php
- **Video Tutorial Link –** http://www.ehow.com/video_2201966_register-join-facebook.html

Who They Are And What They Do – Facebook is a free-access social networking site. Maybe you have been holding out on joining Facebook — but for ORM (Online Reputation Management) purposes, Facebook is a great place to be.

Facebook is the largest social network on the planet and has hundreds of millions of members. Facebook is ranked as the 3rd most visited website in the world by Alexa.com [2]

Facebook is also in the top 10 websites in almost every major country. Because Facebook is ranked so highly and contains so many members who all use their real names, search engines greatly value its information.

---

[2] (http://www.alexa.com/siteinfo/facebook.com).

Within days of opening an account on Facebook your profile information should appear within the top 5 pages for Google searches under your name.

LinkedIn.com

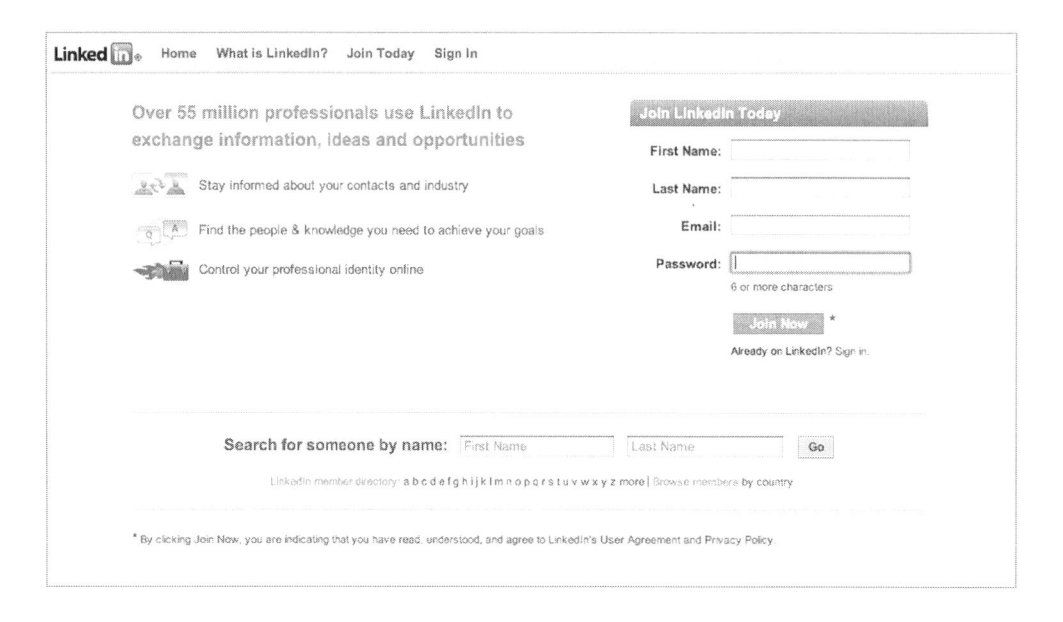

- **Website Link –** http://www.linkedin.com
- **Join Link –** https://www.linkedin.com/reg/join
- **Video Tutorial Link –** http://www.youtube.com watch?v=gelyu0xLCh0

Who They Are And What They Do – With more than 45 million users, and representing 150 industries around the world, LinkedIn is a fast-growing professional networking site that allows members to add business contacts, search for jobs, and find potential clients.

Individuals have the ability to create a professional profile that can be viewed by others in the network; you can also view the profiles of your LinkedIn contacts.

Twitter.com

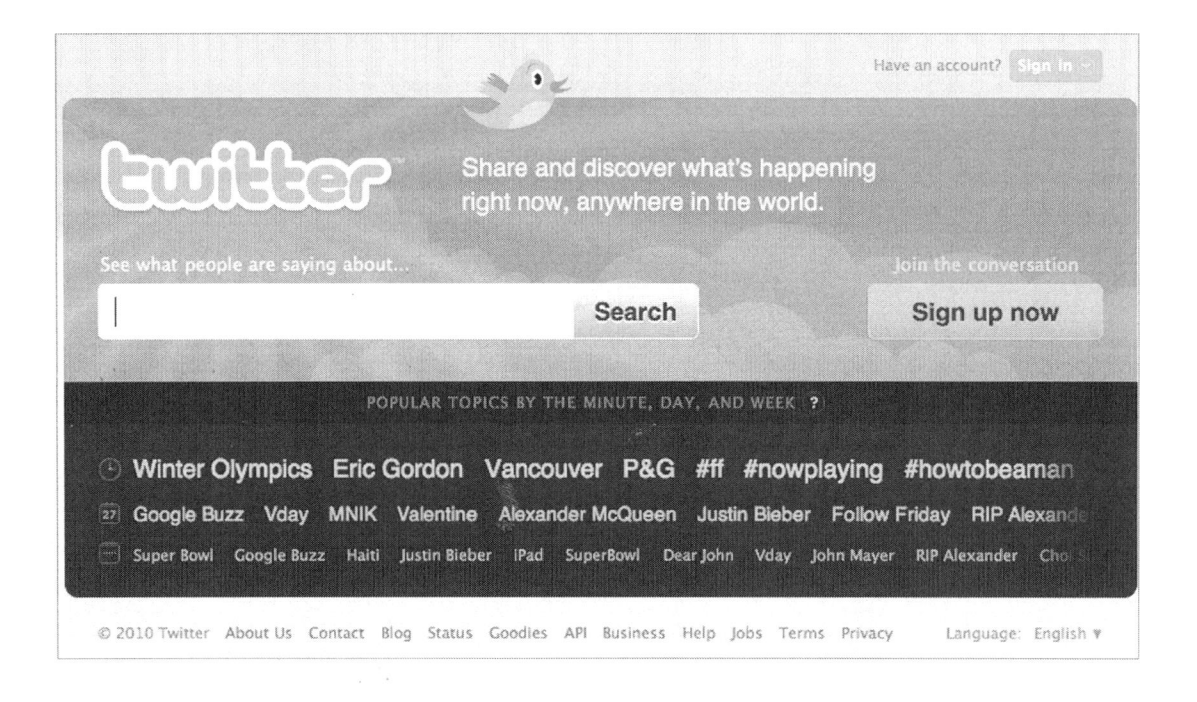

- **Website Link –** http://twitter.com
- **Join Link –** https://twitter.com/signup
- **Video Tutorial Link –** http://www.youtube.com/watch?v=J0xbjIE8cPM

Who They Are And What They Do – Twitter is a free social networking and micro-blogging service that enables its users to send and read messages known as tweets. Tweets are text-based posts of up to 140 characters displayed on the author's profile page and delivered to the author's subscribers — known as followers.

Senders can restrict delivery to those in a circle of friends or, by default, allow open access. Users can send and receive tweets via the Twitter website, Short Message Service (SMS) or external applications.

ZoomInfo.com

- **Website Link** – http://www.zoominfo.com
- **Join Link** – http://www.zoominfo.com/Registration/Register.aspx

Who They Are And What They Do – ZoomInfo is the premier business information search engine, with profiles on more than 45 million people and 5 million companies. ZoomInfo delivers fresh and organized information on industries, companies, people, products, services and jobs.

The Terrific Twenty – Join These Too

- Amazon
- BigSight
- BusinessCard2
- ClaimId
- Digg
- FriendFeed
- GetGlue
- HuffingtonPost
- Identi.ca
- MeetUp
- MyBlogLog
- Naymz
- PeoplePond
- Posterous
- RedOrbit
- SVWsticker
- TheWuffieBank
- TumblR
- Vimeo

Amazon.com

- **Website Link – www.amazon.com**

Who They Are And What They Do – Amazon.com is America's largest online retailer. Amazon has steadily branched into retail sales of music CDs, videotapes and DVDs, software, consumer electronics,
kitchen items, tools, lawn and garden items, toys & games, baby products, apparel, sporting goods, gourmet food, jewelry, watches, health and personal-care items, beauty products, musical instruments, clothing, industrial & scientific supplies, groceries, and more.

Selling so many products has also led to Amazon creating a customer review section whereby Amazon members can share views on each purchased items. Amazon guidelines suggest a theme of "what would you have wanted to know before you purchased the product?" Reviews are suggested at 75 and 300 words.

BigSight.org

- **Website Link –** <u>http://bigsight.org</u>
- **Join Link –** http://bigsight.org/profile/basic

Who They Are And What They Do – BigSight differs from other people search sites by focusing on the creation of a centralized repository of profile information rather than crawling the web to collect personal information from disparate sources.

As such, 87% of BigSight.org profiles appear at the top of Google.

This allows you to share your story with the world. It also differs from resources by encouraging the creation of profiles for any and everyone, not just people who clear a subjective "prominence" bar.

Users are encouraged to update public profiles every quarter, and profiles that go untouched for more than two quarters risk removal from the directory.

Businesscard2.com

- **Website Link** – http://businesscard2.com/
- **Join Link** – http://businesscard2.com/signup

Who They Are And What They Do – BusinessCard2 is an online service that helps professionals network and exchange business cards on the Internet without face to face interaction. BusinessCard2 enables professionals to create, control and leverage their professional online identity via a portable and interactive online business card. BusinessCard2 was created to bridge the gap between traditional business and sales processes that occur in the real world with virtual processes on the Internet.

ClaimId.com

- **Website Link – http://claimid.com**
- **Join Link – https://claimid.com/register**

Who They Are And What They Do – ClaimID is a free and easy way to set yourself up with an OpenID. One of the greatest things about having a ClaimID page is that you can easily provide people searching for you with a real picture of your identity.

With ClaimID you can claim your blog, your website and news articles that mention your name into a central place. If someone is searching for you, they previously might not have found all of those important pages. With ClaimID, you can put your best face forward and let people see the identity you wish to present.

Digg.com

- **Website Link –** <http://digg.com/>
- **Join Link –** <http://digg.com/register>
- **Video Tutorial Link –** http://www.youtube.com/watch?v=NxINcMtcXqU

Who They Are And What They Do – Digg is a social news website made for people to discover and share content from anywhere on the Internet, by submitting links and stories, and voting and commenting on submitted links and stories. Voting stories up and down is the site's cornerstone function, respectively called digging and burying. Many stories get submitted every day, but only the most Dugg stories appear on the front page.

Friendfeed.com

- **Website Link –** <http://friendfeed.com>
- **Join Link –** <https://friendfeed.com/account/create>
- **Video Tutorial –** http://www.youtube.com/watch?v=y9TYAGbKhds

Who They Are And What They Do – Friendfeed enables you to discover and discuss the interesting stuff your friends find on the web. You can create groups and store them as a mailing list. It's an easy way to share baby photos or post funny YouTube videos or you can create a private group for your company or colleagues to collaborate on a research paper, coordinate an upcoming event or give status updates. You can create an account using your Google, Facebook, or Twitter account. Friendfeed was just purchased by Facebook.

GetGlue.com

- **Website Link –** http://getglue.com
- **Join Link –** http://getglue.com/signup/email
- **Video Tutorial –** http://www.youtube.com/watch?v=udDRJGHPJ4k

Who They Are And What They Do – GetGlue is a service that helps you find your next favorite movie, book, music album or other every day thing. Glue shows you things that you'll like based on your personal tastes, what your friends like, and what's most popular on Glue. When you visit pages about books, movies, music, etc. you can click thumbs-up or thumbs-down on things you like or dislike. Glue will then suggest books, movies, music, etc. that you'll like based on your personal tastes and what your friends like.

Huffingtonpost.com

- **Website Link –** http://www.huffingtonpost.com

Who They Are And What They Do – The Huffington Post is an American liberal news website and aggregated blog founded by Arianna Huffington, featuring various news sources and columnists. The site offers coverage of politics, media, business, entertainment, living, style, the green movement, world news, and comedy, and is a top destination for news, blogs and original content.

Identi.ca

- **Website Link –** <http://identi.ca/>
- **Join Link –** <https://identi.ca/main/register>

Who They Are And What They Do – Identi.ca is a micro-blogging service you can use to write short notices about yourself, where you are, and what you're doing, and those notices will be sent to all your friends and fans. Identi.ca's main goal is to provide a fair and transparent service that preserves users' autonomy. In particular, all the software used for Identi.ca is free and all the data is available under the Creative Commons Attribution license, making it Open Data. Identi.ca's goal is autonomy with the belief that you deserve the right to manage your own on-line presence.

Meetup.com

- **Website Link – <http://www.meetup.com>**
- **Join Link –** http://www.meetup.com/register

Who They Are And What They Do – Meetup is the world's largest network of local groups. Meetup makes it easy for anyone to organize a local group or find one of the thousands already meeting up face-to-face. More than 2,000 groups get together in local communities each day, each one with the goal of improving themselves or their communities. Meetup's mission is to revitalize local community and help people around the world self-organize. Meetup believes that people can change their personal world, or the whole world, by organizing themselves into groups that are powerful enough to make a difference.

MyBlogLog.com

- **Website Link –** http://www.mybloglog.com
- **Join Link –** http://www.mybloglog.com/buzz/join

Who They Are And What They Do – MyBlogLog is a social network for the blogger community. Bloggers sign up for free accounts on MyBlogLog and can initiate a blog community for one or more blogs they author. Other registered members can subscribe to these communities, effectively bookmarking them for future reading and sharing them with their own contacts. MyBlogLog communities revolve around an individual blog registered by that blog's author. These communities have anywhere from a few to thousands of members. Communities that are particularly popular, have the most members or that are brand new are featured on the MyBlogLog Communities page.

Naymz.com

- **Website Link –** http://www.naymz.com

Who They Are And What They Do – Naymz is a powerful tool for any professional looking for a career advance. Naymz professional networking platform allows people to find and discover new connections, opportunities, ideas, and information based on backgrounds and reputations. Best thing about Namyz is that whenever someone looks at your profile, Namyz emails you telling you that "someone" looked at your profile.

PeoplePond.com

- **Website Link –** www.peoplepond.com
- **Join Link –** https://secure.peoplepond.com/register.php

Who They Are And What They Do – PeoplePond gives you access to advanced personal identity verification and online service authentication so you can create a trusted platform from which to promote your personal brand. PeoplePond also enables you to demonstrate to your followers that you are who you say you are and that your social media accounts, blogs and other online assets are really yours, not created by someone else trying to spoof your identity.

Posterous.com

- **Website Link –** http://posterous.com
- **Join Link –** http://posterous.com/main/register

Who They Are And What They Do – Posterous is a web publishing platform via email. Text and files can be uploaded to the site via email. Users are not required to create an account to use Posterous.

To start, users simply email content to post@posterous.com and a "blog" is auto-created and sent back to the user. Registered users can tailor the blog URL, post via the website, subscribe to other users.

Posterous embeds video, MP3s and other media into a player and turns images into image galleries. PDFs and other office documents are displayed in a Scribd embedded widget. Users can also add friends and family's email address to any Posterous site they control. When the emails have been added, users can post by sending content they want to publish to post@sitename.posterous.com.

RedOrbit.com

- **Website Link –** http://www.redorbit.com
- **Join Link –** http://www.redorbit.com/join

Who They Are And What They Do – RedOrbit was launched with the goal of creating the largest, most unique Internet community, with the strongest consumer brand, in the most underserved niche on the Web — science. RedOrbit.com has since become the premier Internet destination for space, science, health, and technology enthusiasts around the globe.

RedOrbit.com is committed to providing stimulating, original content and presentation, with over 1,500,000 pages covering the vast ideological spectrums of space, science, health, and technology. With subject matter a bit more intellectually oriented than most, the average RedOrbit.com visitors tend to be well educated, between the ages of 25 - 55, with a median income significantly higher than that of Internet users as a whole.

SVWsticker.com

- **Website Link – http://www.svwsticker.com**
- **Join Link – http://www.svwsticker.com/user/register**

Who They Are And What They Do – SVWsticker is Source Value Wiki online article directory for both publishers and authors that encourages you to weigh the benefits of developing your own article directory and to build a quality resource with value backlink to your site.

TheWuffieBank.org

- **Website Link – http://thewhuffiebank.org**

Who They Are And What They Do – The Whuffie Bank is a nonprofit organization dedicated to building a new currency based on reputation that could be redeemed for real and virtual products and services. The higher your reputation, the wealthier you are. The Wuffie bank wants to build an open organization that aims to measure and enable the exchange of online reputation. The value of your Whuffie is obtained from your online reputation by tracking your interactions with social networks and the feedback from your contacts.

Tumblr.com

- **Website Link –** <http://www.tumblr.com>
- **Join Link –** <http://www.tumblr.com/register>
- **Video Tutorial Link –** <http://www.viddler.com/explore/centernetworks/videos/23>

Who They Are And What They Do — Tumblr is a blogging platform that allows users to post text, images, video, links, quotes, and audio to a "tumblelog" — a short-form blog. Users are able to "follow" other users and see posts together on a dashboard. You can link or reblog other blogs on the site and other users can do the same to your posts. The service emphasizes customizability and ease of use.

Vimeo.com

- **Website Link –** http://www.vimeo.com
- **Join Link –** http://www.vimeo.com/join

Who They Are And What They Do – Vimeo is a video-centric social network site owned by IAC/InterActiveCorp. The site supports embedding, sharing, video storage, and allows user-commenting on each video page. Users must register to upload content. Registered users may also create a profile and upload small user pictures as avatar comments and "like" videos. Vimeo does not allow commercial videos, gaming videos, pornography or anything not created by the user to be hosted on the site. Vimeo has gained a reputation as catering to a high end, artistic crowd because of its higher bitrate resolution and relative HD support.

More Websites You Should Join

For most people, the previous 25 website profile accounts created should provide ample material to create a large portion of search results. If you feel you want to continue, the following websites can also be used to build profiles. These websites typically do not rank as well as highly on search engines as the previous 25. However, each online reputation situation is different and many of these may actually work better for your online presence then the previous 25 listed, so give them a try.

- ActiveRain.com – The largest online gathering of real estate professionals in the world.

- Agentb.com – A place for you to find and share great deals from across the Internet.

- BigStartUps.com – An online community of startup companies who want to share their experiences.

- Biznik.com – A social community for business.

- BlinkList.com – A social bookmarking site that is easy to pick up and use for the beginner.

- BlogCatalog.com – A blogger social network and directory to help bloggers connect, share ideas.

- BlogFlux.com – Designed to be a central destination for the blogosphere.

- Classmates.com – A social networking service — you can add basic information for free.

- CoComment.com – A service for managing conversations online and keeping track of comments

- Connotea.org – Free online reference management and sharing for researchers and scientists.

- coRank.com – The place to create pages where you can add things you find interesting on the web.

- Curbly.com – The best DIY, craft, home improvement and interior design community.

- Deals.com – Find and share and post discounts, sales and deals Docstoc.com is a community for people to find and share professional documents.

- DotNetKicks.com – A community that specializes in .NET development techniques, technologies and tools.

- Diigo.com – A powerful research tool and a knowledge-sharing community.

- Elance.com – Outsource to expert programmers, designers, coders, writers, developers.

- Epinons.com – Consumer-generated reviews, buying tips and advice.

- Faves.com – Social bookmarking.

- Friendster.com – A global social network to meet new people through friends.

- Guru.com – Search 100000+ freelance programmers, web developers, graphic designers, and more.

- HubPages.com – An online space to share your advice, reviews, useful tips, opinions and insights.

- Imeem.com – A social music service.

- Indianpad.com – A user edited bookmark of news stories.

- Jaiku.com – Create your own microblog and connect with your friends.

- Jigsaw.com – A prospecting tool used by sales professionals, marketers and recruiters.

- Kaching.com – An investing talent marketplace where investors can get access to the investing talent.

- Kirtsy.com – A social media platform to find cool things.

- Last.fm – The world's largest online music catalogue, with free music streaming, videos.

- LiveJournal.com – A free service for journaling and blogging, offering privacy and photo storage.

- Mixx.com – User-recommendations for stories, photos and videos MetaCafe.com — One of the world's largest video sites, serving the videos, movies and clips.

- MyLife.com – Comprehensive people search service.

- MySpace.com – A leading worldwide social network that offers customization of your profile.

- Netvouz.com – A social bookmark manager where you can store your favorite links online.

- oDesk.com – A global service marketplace to hire, manage, and pay remote freelancers.

- Plaxo.com – Your online address book.

- Plime.com – An editable wiki community where users can add and edit weird and interesting links.

- Plurk.com – A social journal for your life.

- Propeller.com – A social news portal, programmed its' audience.

- Quizilla.com – A user generated online quiz website.

- Reddit.com – User-generated news links. Votes promote stories to the front page.

- Simpy.com – A social bookmarking service that lets you save, tag, search and share bookmarks.

- Squidoo.com – A community website that allows users to create pages for subjects of interest.

- Spout.com – It offers movie reviews, movie ratings, film details, synopsis, summary and new movie trailers.

- Stumbleupon.com – Free browser extension which acts as an browsing tool for sharing web sites.

- Technorati.com – Real-time search for user-generated media (including weblogs).

- Toluu.com – Makes it easy to share your feeds with friends and discover new feeds.

- TripAdvisor.com – A free travel website that gathers and shares travel information from its' members.

- Vois.com – The first social network dedicated to bringing together talent with the right opportunities.

- Wink.com – A people search engine.

- Xing.com – Business networking for professionals.

- Yedda.com – Finding the best answers from the most relevant people. Just for you.

- YouNoodle.com – A place to discover and support the hottest early-stage companies and people.

- ZiiTrend.com – A home for future predictions. Discover the power of social prediction with other users.

- Zimbio.com – an Interactive Magazine.

- Zooomr.com – is a social utility to communicate securely through photos and text messages in realtime.

- 43things.com – A social networking site where users create accounts and then share lists of goals and hopes

Chapter 6
Photo Sharing Can Also Fix Your Reputation

Adding Pictures Can Improve Your Reputation

Sharing photos on your website or the Internet is a great way to get positive attention from Google and other search engines. As you learned in profile building, adding a photo is very important as those photos regularly get crawled by spiders and then are added to search engines.

In many cases photo sharing websites perform even better in searches. While there are many websites to which you can upload photos, very few actually rank high in search positioning or image positioning. When posting photos, again remember to use only the photos that put you in the best light. The two best sites for reputation management in photo sharing are:

- Flickr
- Photobucket

Flickr.com

- **Website Link – http://www.flickr.com**
- **Tour Link –** http://www.flickr.com/tour

Flickr is an image and video hosting website, web services suite, and online community platform. In addition to being a popular website for users to share personal photographs, the service is widely used by bloggers as a photo repository.

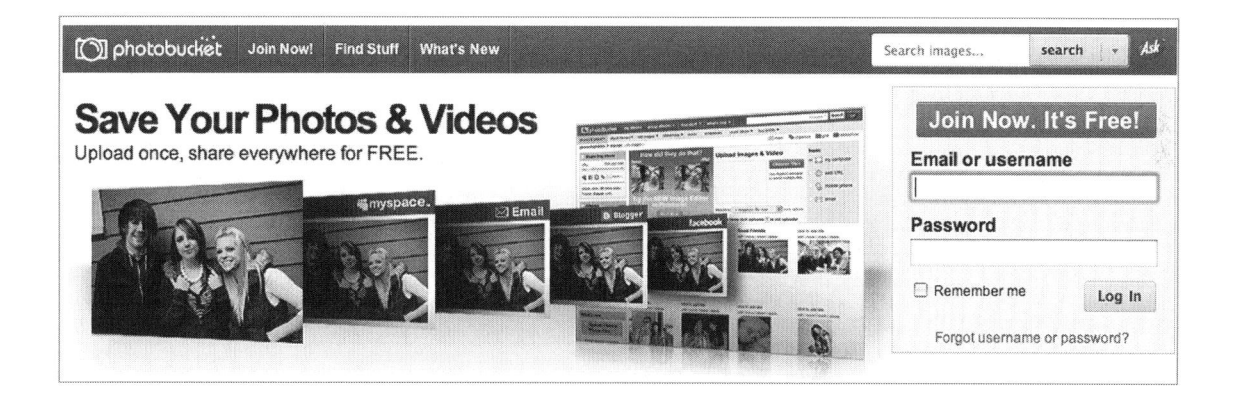

Photobucket.com

- **Website Link –** http://photobucket.com
- **Join Link –** http://register.photobucket.com

Photobucket is a site on the Internet for uploading, sharing, linking and finding photos, videos and graphics. Your free Photobucket account can store thousands of photos and hours of video.

Chapter 7
Video Sharing Can Also Fix Your Reputation

How Posting Videos Can Improve Your Reputation

Recently Google changed the algorithms — the mathematical formulas they use to determine organic web rankings. And with the change, the greatest mathematical value was placed on videos.

Consequently, one of the best steps you can take to improve your online reputation is adding videos to the Internet. Because video is such a popular Internet component, video links and clips often get spidered by search engines every few minutes and videos often appear in search engines like Google, Yahoo and MSN just minutes after submission — as opposed to the days or weeks non-video content takes to be ranked on search engines.

Begin by making a simple video including your domain name at the beginning of your description and your name within the description. Then submit your video to sites like YouTube where Google can quickly pick it up.

For greater exposure, submit your videos to multiple video distribution sites like TubeMogul which can distribute video content to as many as 12 search engines at once. This often can have your video appear alongside organic search listings on the first few pages of many search engines.

YouTube.com

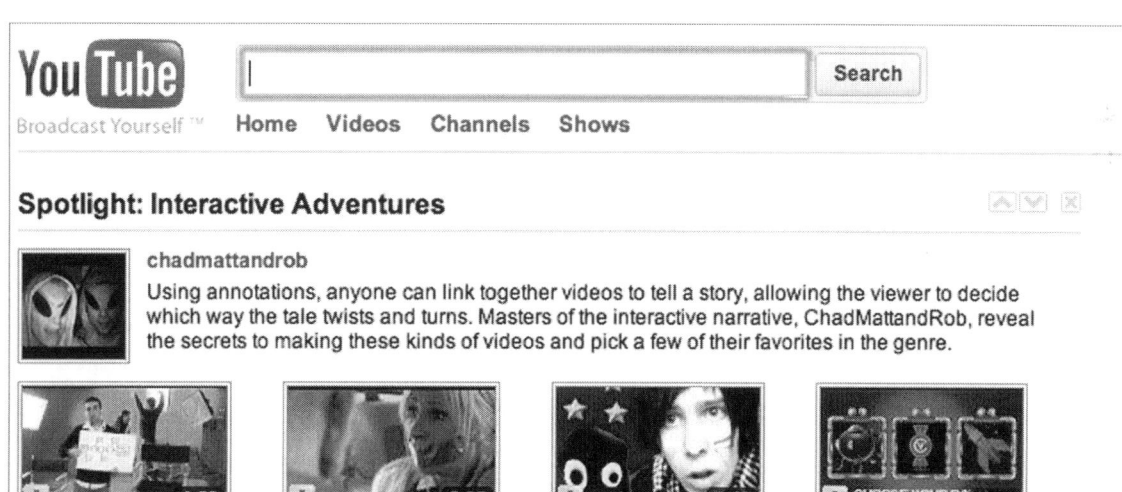

Spotlight: Interactive Adventures

chadmattandrob
Using annotations, anyone can link together videos to tell a story, allowing the viewer to decide which way the tale twists and turns. Masters of the interactive narrative, ChadMattandRob, reveal the secrets to making these kinds of videos and pick a few of their favorites in the genre.

How To Make An Interactive Adven...
1 week ago
81,475 views
chadmattandrob

The Birthday Party: An Interacti...
1 month ago
357,081 views
chadmattandrob

INTERACTIVE SPACE ADVENTURE
8 months ago
190,891 views
AmazingPhil

VLOGCANDY INTERACTIVE
1 week ago
45,929 views
VlogCandy

- **Website Link –** <u>http://www.youtube.com/</u>
- **Join Link –** http://www.youtube.com/create_account

With YouTube you can join the largest worldwide video-sharing community. This will permit you to:

- Search and browse millions of community and partner videos
- Comment, rate, and make video responses to your favorite videos
- Upload and share your videos with millions of other users
- Save your favorite videos to watch and share later

TubeMogul.com

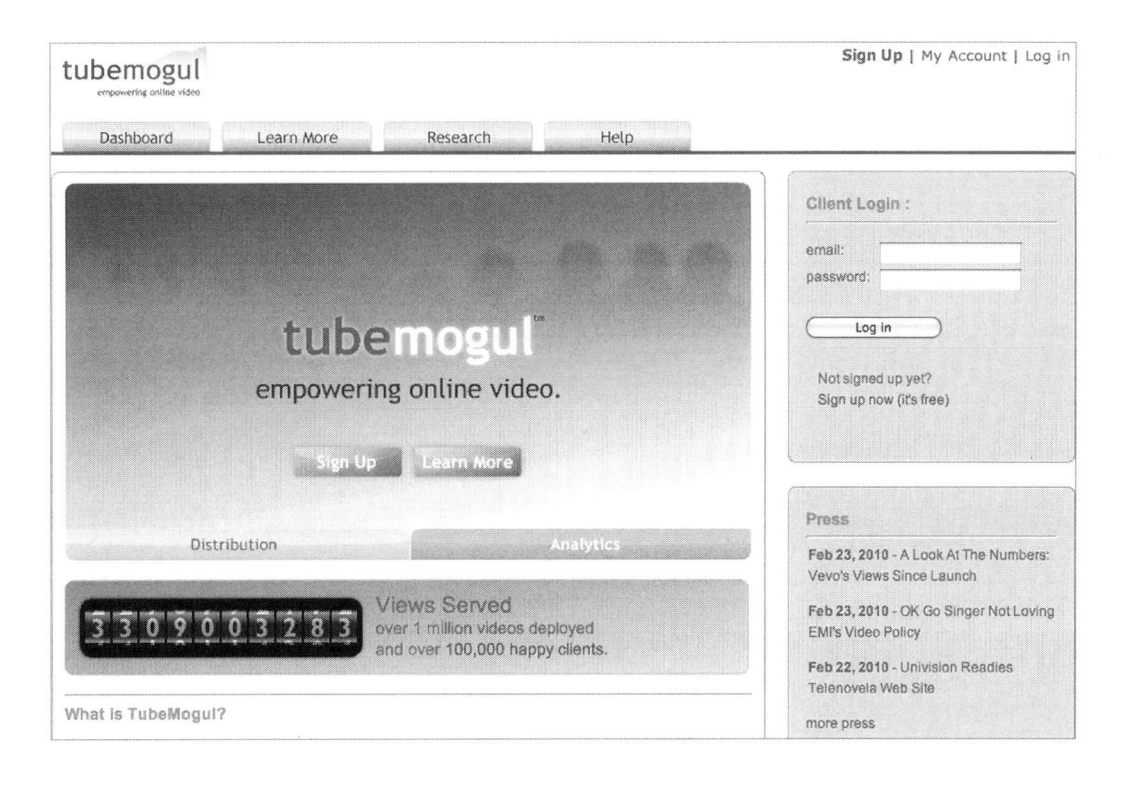

- **Website Link –** http://tubemogul.com
- **Join Link –** http://www.tubemogul.com/signup

If you are launching a video campaign, use tubemogul.com. TubeMogul is a free service that provides a single point for deploying uploads to the top video sharing sites. It also offers powerful analytics on who, what, and how videos are being viewed. This will distribute your one video to over 12 different video search engines like Vimeo, Revver, Daily Motion, Break.com and Imeem with the push of a button. TubeMogul tracks rich, standardized analytics far beyond "views". These include per-second audience drop-off, audience geography and much more.

Chapter 8
Domain Names and Websites

Do You Own Your Own Name?

When we ask most people if they own their name as a domain name what surprises us most is the majority say no. The first thing you should do right now is purchasing your name as a domain name. It doesn't matter if you're not ready to start a website — the important thing is to make sure that you own your name.

A domain name and a website are different. The website is the content — articles, images and files that make up the website — while the domain name is just the address — the right to have, "amazon.com" or "stockmarket.com" that can point users to your website.

The best domain names reflect a company's brand. If someone is interested in

Toyota automobiles, they'll typically type "Toyota" into Google, or just try "www.toyota.com" in the browser. This is known as "Type-in traffic".

As an individual, your brand is your name. Thus, if your name is Martin Mcallistaer, your ideal domain name is going to be "martinmcallistaer.com". Maybe your friends call you Marty. In that case, "martymcallistaer.com" would be a close second. If that's the case take both names, if they are available.

Like you, every domain name is unique. There can't be two websites called "Amazon.com" on the Internet. This means that if somebody else registers your name as a domain before you do, you'll never be able to use it. The easiest way to check if your name is available as a domain is to look on a website like Godaddy — www.godaddy.com, and point to see if your name domain is available. If you cannot get your name with a .com suffix you may be able to get the ".net" equivalent, or the ".me", or one of the many other types of domain suffixes, but the .com is clearly the most powerful and most preferable.

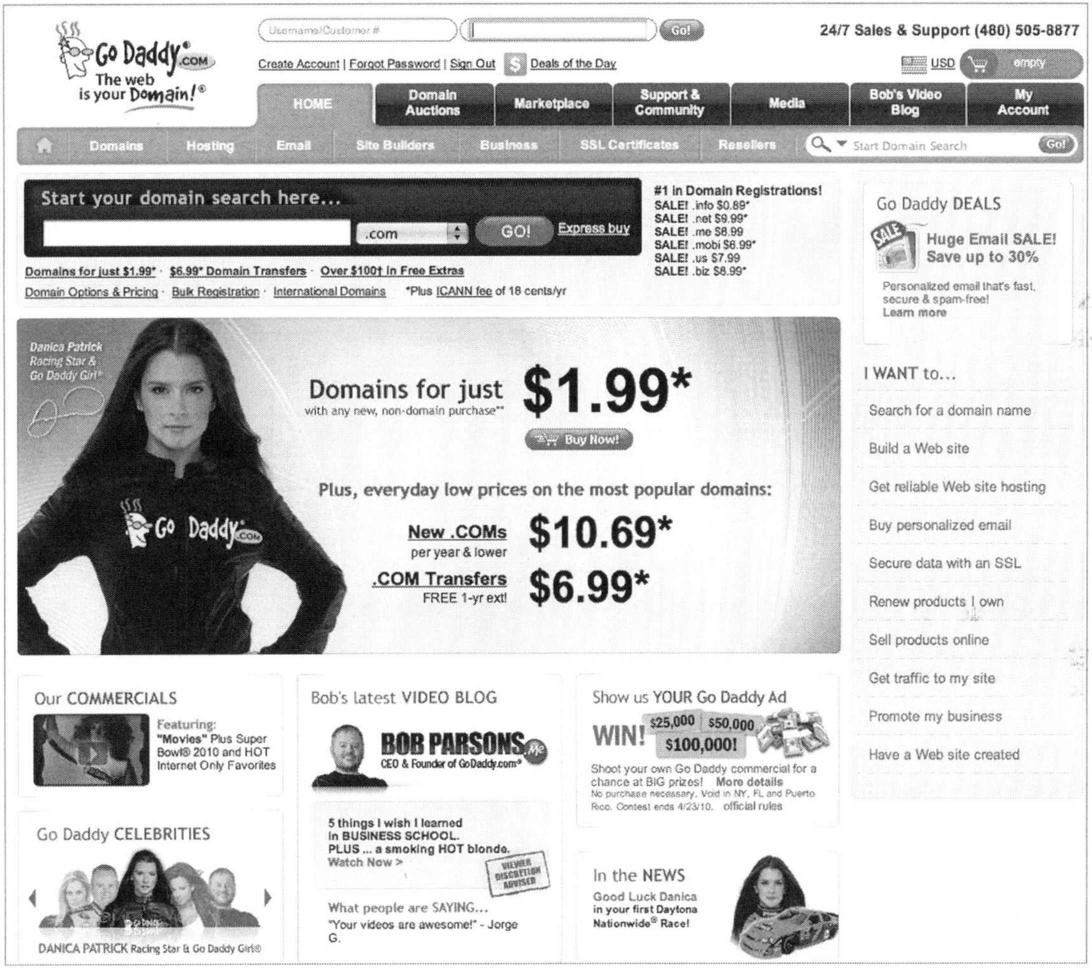
Go Daddy.com
The web is your Domain!®
Create Account | Forgot Password | Sign Out
Deals of the Day
24/7 Sales & Support (480) 505-8877
USD
empty
HOME
Domain Auctions
Marketplace
Support & Community
Media
Bob's Video Blog
My Account
Domains
Hosting
Email
Site Builders
Business
SSL Certificates
Resellers
Start Domain Search
Start your domain search here...
.com
GO!
Express buy
#1 in Domain Registrations!
SALE! .info $0.89*
SALE! .net $9.99*
SALE! .me $8.99
SALE! .mobi $6.99*
SALE! .us $7.99
SALE! .biz $8.99*
Domains for just $1.99* · $6.99* Domain Transfers · Over $100† in Free Extras
Domain Options & Pricing · Bulk Registration · International Domains *Plus ICANN fee of 18 cents/yr
Go Daddy DEALS
Huge Email SALE! Save up to 30%
Personalized email that's fast, secure & spam-free!
Learn more
Danica Patrick Racing Star & Go Daddy Girl®
Domains for just $1.99*
with any new, non-domain purchase**
Buy Now!
Plus, everyday low prices on the most popular domains:
New .COMs $10.69*
per year & lower
.COM Transfers $6.99*
FREE 1-yr ext!
I WANT to...
Search for a domain name
Build a Web site
Get reliable Web site hosting
Buy personalized email
Secure data with an SSL
Renew products I own
Sell products online
Get traffic to my site
Promote my business
Have a Web site created
Our COMMERCIALS
Featuring: "Movies" Plus Super Bowl® 2010 and HOT Internet Only Favorites
Bob's latest VIDEO BLOG
BOB PARSONS.me
CEO & Founder of GoDaddy.com®
5 things I wish I learned in BUSINESS SCHOOL.
PLUS ... a smoking HOT blonde.
Watch Now >
VIEWER DISCRETION ADVISED
What people are SAYING...
"Your videos are awesome!" - Jorge G.
Show us YOUR Go Daddy Ad
WIN! $25,000 $50,000 $100,000!
Shoot your own Go Daddy commercial for a chance at BIG prizes! More details
No purchase necessary. Void in NY, FL and Puerto Rico. Contest ends 4/23/10. official rules
Go Daddy CELEBRITIES
DANICA PATRICK Racing Star & Go Daddy Girl®
In the NEWS
Good Luck Danica in your first Daytona Nationwide® Race!

If your name is Martin Mcallistaer, but another person named Martin Mcallistaer decides to buy martinmcallistaer.com, and builds a website, he may well have a stronger web presence than you will if your name is also Martin Mcallistaer. He will certainly get all of the "type-in" traffic.

Owning your own personal name as a domain name is one of the most important things you can do in owning your online reputation. If you get your name now, and secure it, then whenever you're ready to launch your website, you'll be in a strong position to start building a strong Internet presence.

Domain registration itself is more like renting than buying: when you pay your money, it isn't for the permanent use of the name. What you're paying for is the right to exclusive use of that name for as many years as you agree to buy.

It's best to select "auto-renew" when you first purchase so that when that time runs out, your domain will re-register. The auto-renew will charge your credit card, but in the meantime you won't lose the right to use the name.

If you don't auto-renew, or pay for renewal yourself before the name registration expires, then the name is released back into the domain name marketplace, and anyone can then buy the right to use it.

The good news is that domain names are relatively inexpensive. Registering a domain name is only going to cost about $10 per year. Domain names are registered with companies called registrars. These are the companies that perform the registration for you, and maintain your details.

GoDaddy is perhaps the best known registrar. Be sure to keep all of the confirmation emails from the registrar, as these contain important information. Once you've got the domain name, you can start working on your new website, create a temporary, basic website with just a couple of pages of information, or just leave it blank until you're ready. The important thing is that you've got that domain name secured, and it's yours for whenever you need it.

I Own My Own Name. Now What?

Once you own your name as a domain name, the best thing you can do is have that domain point to information about yourself that you want the world to see.

Maybe you have a corporate profile from your company website and that is the information you want the world to see. In that case simply have the domain company point the link to that URL — or perhaps an existing blog.

However in most cases individuals will have to create a website or blog page to represent what the domain name will show to the world — and that can be done by a professional website developer, or you can do it yourself.

We know the idea of creating a website yourself might sound daunting but in reality with today's tools it's very easy. One of the easiest ways to create a website is actually through GoDaddy.

GoDaddy has a product called Website Tonight.

113

It's probably the easiest Website creation tool on the Internet. You can build your own website in minutes. While it is easy to use this GoDaddy tool, remember it has a minimal cost to start and small monthly fees as well for each month you host your site with GoDaddy.

Other free options include blog formation with blogs from companies like Blogger and WordPress that we will discuss in Chapter 9 and other free website development options such as Weebly — www.weebly.com .

Weebly's basic service is free and basic website development and hosting is free as well. Weebly is also pretty easy to navigate. It's not as easy as GoDaddy's Website Tonight — and involves a little bit technical follow through regarding domain pointing — but if you want a free website creation option for beginners this would be the one to choose.

weebly
web creation made easy

Username
Password
☑ Remember Me | Forgot PW   **log in**

Home | Features | Blog | Support | About Us | Contact Us

Create a free website.
Fast. Free. Easy. Now.

Username
Password
Email

☐ I accept the terms of service

Sign Up

PLAY DEMO

What can I do with Weebly?

- Create a free website & blog
- Easy drag and drop interface
- No technical skills required
- Dozens of professional designs
- Free domain hosting

GigaOM says:
The simplicity and ease of use of their new blogging feature is stunning.

Featured Sites
www.Vellephant.com
Unforgettable Freelance Design for Web & Print.
Atlanta, GA

Weebly for Education
We just released Weebly for Education.
Check it out.

Features | About Us | Contact Us | Jobs | Affiliates | Developers | Blog | Terms Of Service | Privacy | Support
©2010 Weebly, Inc.

Google "Insurance"?

This might seem extreme but some Online Reputation Specialists believe that owning all the domain names that contain your "exact name" is the best way to disarm an angry detractor.

The tech slang name for this policy is "Google Insurance". The fact is that owning your name and all its extensions — think johndoe.com, johndoe.net, johndoe.cc, johndoe.me, etc — will make it much harder for a detractor to leapfrog to the top search of your exact name if you own them but there are no guarantees.

Some clever detractors are wise to this move and resort to variants of your domain with your name contained within the variant. So if your name was Martin Mcallistaer and you own MartinMcallistaer.com your detractor might create MartinMcallistaerSucks.com as a blog and start posting to it.

Unfortunately, this move can be effective for the detractor if a strong online reputation campaign is not in place. Regardless of the variant, a domain with your name contained within it can act as a strong magnet for search engines and that's why some reputation specialists recommend taking a few variants of your name — with sucks as a suffix as well.

We feel that this is extreme for most individuals simply looking to build a good reputation campaign. However, if you have many detractors you should take the time to buy up these other domains and extensions. That is particularly true for domains related to a business. With a variant of your business name as a domain name, an angry employee can cause significant havoc.

Chapter 9
Blogs – Your Internet Diary

What is a Blog?

The word blog is a contraction of the term "web log". A Blog is a website where an individual enters commentary or descriptions of events — sort of like an online diary.

Blogs are especially good for online reputation management because search engines love content and blogs provide a lot of that content. Remember search engines rank web pages. Each web page provides a new opportunity to have you rank well. Every time you put up a new blog post, you have another opportunity to be found at Google, Yahoo, or any other search engine.

A typical blog combines text, images and links to other blogs, Web pages, and other media related to its topic. The ability of readers to leave comments in an interactive format is an important part of many blogs. The most popular blog services are:

- WordPress
- Blogger

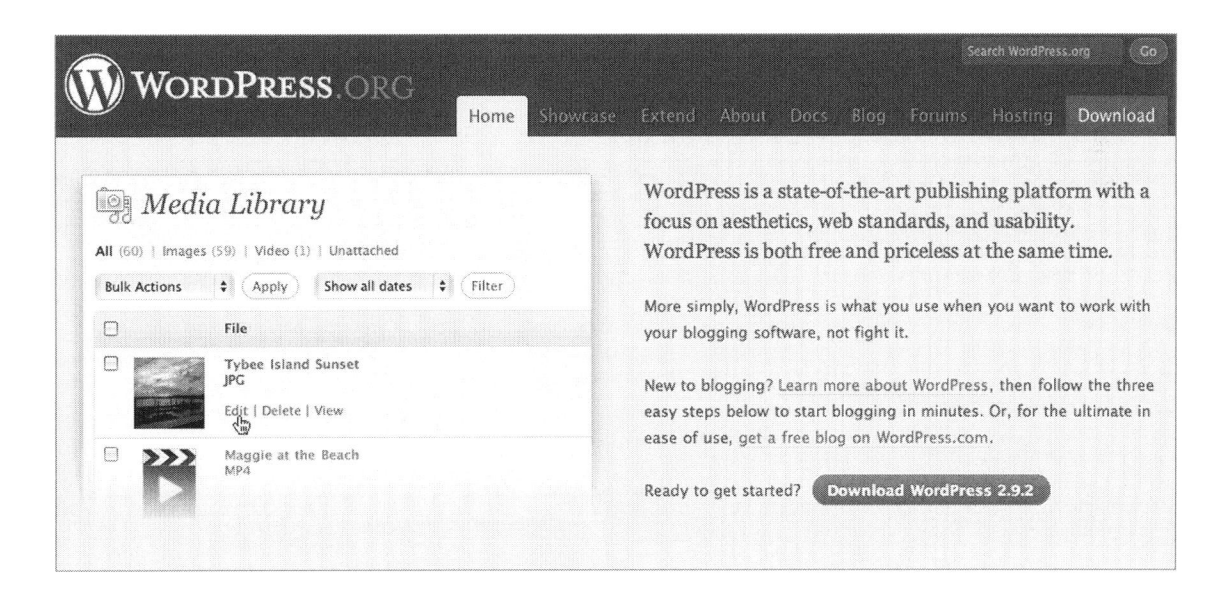

WordPress.com

- **Website Link –** http://wordpress.com
- **Tutorial Link –** http://www.youtube.com/watch?v=H1ImndT0fC8

WordPress is an open source blog publishing application which can also be used for basic content management. It has many features including a user-friendly workflow, a rich plugin architecture, and an advanced templating system.

It was first released in May 2003 and as of September 2009, it is being used by 202 million websites worldwide. WordPress.com lets you get started with a new and free WordPress-based blog in seconds, but varies in several ways and is less flexible than WordPress.org which you download and install yourself.

Blogger.com

- **Website Link –** https://www.blogger.com/start
- **Tutorial Link –** http://www.youtube.com/watch?v=BnploFsS_tY

Creating your blog with Blogger takes just a few easy steps. In a matter of minutes you can start posting text, photos, videos, and more to your blog — and it's free.

Blogger

Language: English

Sign in to use Blogger with your Google Account

Username (Email): Password: (?)

SIGN IN

☐ Remember me (?)

Create a blog. It's free.

CREATE A BLOG

It's easy, and only takes a minute.

Your blog. Share your thoughts, photos, and more with your friends and the world.

Learn more:
- Take a quick tour
- Watch a video tutorial
- Discover more features
- Read Blogger Buzz

Easy to use. It's easy to post text, photos, and videos from the web or your mobile phone.

Blogs of Note

◐◑ The House of Marrakesh

Flexible. Unlimited flexibility to personalize your blog with themes, gadgets, and more.

Home | Features | About | Buzz | Help | Discuss | Language | Developers | Gear
Terms of Service | Privacy | Content Policy | Copyright © 1999 - 2010 Google

Bloggers simple-to-use interface lets you change fonts, bold or italicize your text, adjust text color and alignment, and more. As you compose each new blog post, Blogger saves it automatically, without interrupting your typing. There's also an easy-to-use spell-check feature and a simple way to add labels to your post.
In addition, Blogger includes an HTML editor that lets you fully customize the look and feel of your posts. When you create your blog, you can host it for free on BlogSpot. Just choose an available URL and you're ready to go. If you change your mind and want a different URL later, making the change is easy.

Blogger also includes a custom domain option. You can have a domain name, like example.com, and your blog can still be hosted on by Blogger. You can also add a photo to your blog post by clicking on the image icon in the post editor toolbar. Your photos are then hosted in your free Picasa (from Google) Web Albums account, where you can order prints and organize photos into albums.

Chapter 10
Guest Blogging

Guest blogging is a great way to increase your visibility, bringing visitors to your site. More importantly, it can also be an effective way to improve your online reputation.

What is Guest Blogging?

Guest blogging is a method used by bloggers to increase blog traffic where bloggers write posts to be published on other bloggers' blogs. Guest blogging can work in one of two ways:

- You write a post to appear on another person's blog.
- Another person writes a post to appear on your blog.

Many blogs have a section for guest bloggers. After writing guest posts, you can link back to your site from these guest posts using your name. Quality posts are always welcomed by bloggers. Being a good guest blogger also pulls strong with search engines. Below are some quick tips for being a guest blogger,

Quick Tips

Read the Blog, Don't Just Post! — Your posts are part of your reputation. If you want another blogger to publish your guest post take some time to read through the blog's current content.

Use Your Real Name as a Blogger — If your goal is to build your reputation, use your real name blogging.

Provide Links to Your Blogs and Online Writing — Show the other blogger that you can write intelligently and provide links to your blog

Start Small — Start your guest blogging efforts on smaller blogs, learning the ropes and building your online reputation.

Give Your Best Effort — When writing guest posts, make sure it is your absolute best and absolutely free of spelling and grammatical errors.

Don't Astroturf — Don't overload your posts with links to your own blogs or websites or run the same post over multiple blogs or do other online activities that are similar in nature called "Astroturfing". If your guest post looks like spam because it's covered in links to your own content, then it's likely the post will be rejected.

Promote Your Guest Post — After you guest post - promote it and drive traffic to it.

Chapter 11
Being a Community Member Helps

Just Ask

With millions of users devoted to helping others answer life's biggest — as well as trivial questions and concerns — question and answer communities are quickly filling the net. Because the communities are so active and engaged, many are an Online Reputation Management specialist marketer's dream.

Posting questions and answers on such communities is a good way to get inbound links, target relevant traffic, and establish an online reputation as an expert in your niche. But as mentioned in the last chapter, it's important to actually contribute something because posting random answers with links will not get the results you seek.

Some of The Best Question and Answer Communities are:

- Askville
- Answers
- Yahoo Answers

Askville.com

- **Website Link: http://askville.amazon.com/Index.do**

Askville is a user-driven research site founded by Amazon.com. Unlike other question-answer sites, Askville has evolved into a social community as well as an information site. This is primarily because discussion boards are there where members can enter into long discussions, sparked by individual questions.

Answers.com

- **Website link: <http://www.answers.com>**

Answers.com is a website that presents content gathered from other reference websites. Answers.com marries the best of community-driven questions and answers with hundreds of respected and trusted editorial reference books. The site gets the best answer to give you, whether it summons the expansive, ever-growing collection of community answers from WikiAnswers, or it taps into its ReferenceAnswers database, a comprehensive set of editorial, licensed reference topics.

Yahoo! Answers

- **Website link – http://answers.yahoo.com**

Yahoo! Answers is a community-driven Q&A site that allows users to both submit questions to be answered, and answer questions asked by other users. The site gives members the chance to earn points as a way to encourage participation. The site has often been criticized as being more about social networking than providing accurate information — and that questions seeking factual information received few and usually simplistic answers.

Chapter 12
Using Pay-Per-Post Blogs Sites

Paid Bloggers Can Quickly Help

When trying to augment your online reputation, doesn't a small army of bloggers in your corner sound like a dream come true?

As you know from the headline above, where there's a buck, there's a blog writer waiting to claim it. There are companies that will supply you with a small army of bloggers, ready to march on your command.

Very often these blog posts will quickly show up in your online reputation campaign. To begin, you can try one or more of the companies below. A suggestion would be to have the bloggers evaluate your new website, or something that is trivial, so the bloggers are limited in scope on what they are blogging.

Some of the blogger firms are:

SponsoredReviews.com

- **Website Link –** http://www.sponsoredreviews.com/
- **Join Link –** http://www.sponsoredreviews.com/create-account.asp

SponsoredReviews is a blog advertising network that allows members to build links, increase traffic, and improve search engine rankings on your website. This firm has tens of thousands of independent bloggers who will write blog reviews about your site.

PayPerPost.com

- **Website Link –** http://payperpost.com

PayPerPost delivers online word-of-mouth marketing, brand building and traffic generation through the world's largest consumer generated advertising community and marketplace. PayPerPost is a self-serve easy application service that allows advertisers to reach out to its own network of over 265,000 bloggers — known as "Posties".

Posties review, promote and market products, services and websites on behalf of PayPerPost advertisers. Advertisers on PayPerPost set a single fee — paid to all bloggers regardless of size.

ReviewMe.com

- **Website Link –** http://www.reviewme.com

ReviewMe has a somewhat different model than PayPerPost. Where advertisers on PayPerPost set a single fee — paid to all bloggers and regardless of size — ReviewMe uses an algorithm based on Alexa, Technorati and other statistics to determine the importance of a blog and charges a different fee for each blog based on that calculation.

Blogger payments can range from $30 — $1,000 per post. Also, Bloggers must disclose that the blog review is a paid advertisement, i.e., "The following is a paid review:" "Paid Advertisement:" etc.

This is another improvement over PayPerPost, which is heavily criticized because it does not require disclosure. Finally, advertisers can purchase posts, but cannot require that a post is positive. The blogger can choose to write an honest opinion without fear of not being paid. The only requirement is that the review must be a minimum of 200 words.

LoudLaunch.com

- **Website Link –** http://www.loudlaunch.com/Default.aspx
- **Join Link –** https://www.loudlaunch.com/Users/Register.aspx

The LoudLaunch Team has more than 20 years combined experience in Internet marketing, promotion, Internet technologies, and content creation. Recognizing the importance of measuring marketing ROI and marketing effectiveness, LoudLaunch has invested substantially in developing the services and campaign management tools necessary to help you improve your long term search ranking as part of a broader SEO strategy.

LoudLaunch delivers your controlled message directly into the blogosphere via its network of online publishers. With LoudLaunch you set objectives, establish requirements, and include links and pictures (optional). Its network of publishers will write a campaign that will be based on your stated objectives and requirements.

Chapter 13
How To Use Press Releases in ORM

Your Friend – The Media

Search engines love media. In fact, engines like it so much nowadays that "regular" search results are more and more being replaced with images, videos and news clippings — but let's start with the paper.

Using Press Releases

Press releases can help you improve your online image. By launching an online press release campaign you can funnel in much needed positive press. Many reputation management firms have been using this approach to clean up and improve client online branding.

What is a Press Release?

Press releases are statements prepared for distribution to the news media, announcing something with the intent of gaining media coverage. Press releases:

- Increase your visibility in search engines.
- Indirectly bring traffic to your website, enhancing the link popularity.
- Build brand image.
- Have strong staying power with search engines.

How To Create a Press Release

All press releases contain the following six elements:

- Headline — The headline is the first line of text in a press release and tells what the press release is about.

- Dateline — The dateline contains the release date of the press release and the originating city of the press release.
- Introduction — Is the first paragraph in a press release that generally gives basic answers to the questions of who, what, when, and where.
- Body — The body comes after the introduction further explaining, statistics, background, or other details relevant to the news outlined in the introductory paragraph.
- About — The about section is also called the "boilerplate" as it used over and over again. It is generally a short section at the end of your press release and providing background information on the press release issuing company, organization or individual.
- Media Contact Information — This section contains the name, phone number, email address, mailing address, or other contact information for the media relations contact person.

Still confused? Lets look a press release to see how what you've just read is actually done.

PR Log - Global Press Release Distribution

Fundraising Goals Kick Off the New Year Right

By Solecki Chiropractic
Dated: Jan 05, 2010

Chiropractic office begins raising donations for American Cancer Society.

The Relay For Life is a nation-wide fund-raising event that takes place in cities around the United States annually. All money raised throughout these events in donated to the American Cancer Society to aid in finding a cure. Solecki Chiropractic and Acupuncture has had a team at Weld County's Relay For Life for the past 3 years. This year, the doctors and staff are starting their fund-raising early in hope of collecting twice what they did last year. Dr. Dave Solecki is excited about this coming Relay and the staff can't wait to kick off their fund-raising.

"Cancer is a disease that touches so many lives and we are just happy to be raising funds for such a great cause and event. Our fund-raising will be on-going over the next six months and we have some really fun stuff planned. Not only will we be hosting bake sales every month, but I am even offering to shave my head if the patients and staff can raise $5000 for our team!" stated Dr. Solecki when asked about this years event.

Solecki Chiropractic and Acupuncture encourages any new and existing patients to come into the office and join their team. The office is open a variety of hours and days for scheduling convenience.

###

Solecki Chiropractic and Acupuncture is a comprehensive facility ready to serve the health care needs of you and your family. Drs. Dave and Nicole Solecki are experienced Doctors of Chiropractic and have been in practice for 9 years in Greeley Colorado.

Category	Event, Medical, Health
Tags	chiropractic, cancer, relay, donate, raise, philathropic, life, acupuncture, fund, raising
Email	Click to email author
Phone	(970) 353-2101
Fax	(970) 353-0754
Address	3624 West 10th St
	Greeley, CO 80634
City/Town	Greeley
State/Province	Colorado
Zip	80634
Country	United States

Free and Pay Press Release Services

There are three primary Pay-to-Disseminate Press Release Services:

- PRNewswire
- BusinessWire
- MarketWire

Press Releases from each of these services typically begin at about $200 per release for basic local coverage and can range up to $5,000 each, if released worldwide.

PRNewswire

- **Website Link –** http://www.prnewswire.com

PR Newswire is a global leader in innovative communications and marketing services, enabling organizations to connect and engage with target audiences worldwide.

Through its multi-channel distribution network, audience intelligence, targeting, and measurement services, PR Newswire helps corporations and organizations conduct rich, timely and dynamic dialogues with the media, consumers, policymakers, investors and the general public, in support of building brands, generating awareness, impacting public policy, driving sales, and raising capital.

Pioneering the commercial news distribution industry 55 years ago, PRNewswire connects customers with audiences in more than 170 countries and in over 40 languages through an unparalleled network of offices in 16 countries across North and South America, Europe, Asia, and the Middle East.

PRNewswire is a subsidiary of United Business Media Limited, a global business media company that serves professional commercial communities around the world.

BusinessWire

- **Website Link –** http://www.businesswire.com

Business Wire, a wholly owned subsidiary of Berkshire Hathaway, is a global market leader in commercial news distribution. Thousands of member companies and organizations depend on Business Wire to transmit full-text news releases, regulatory filings, photos and other multimedia content to journalists, financial professionals, investor services, regulatory authorities and the general public worldwide. Business Wire originates hundreds of thousands of news announcements each year, with a dramatic impact on capital and commercial markets around the globe and in virtually every industry sector.

MarketWire

- **Website Link – http://www.marketwire.com**

Marketwire is a newswire service offering press release distribution; media contact management, multimedia, media monitoring services and other workflow solutions for public relations, investor relations, journalists and other communications professionals.

The Free Firms

While you will pay for press release services from the top three firms noted above, there are also the following new, smaller free press services:

- PRLog
- Free-Press-Release
- Craigslist

PRLog.com

- **Website Link – http://www.prlog.org**

PRLog is a free online press release service, including formatting, preview, dedicated web page, pressroom and pdf versions.

Free-Press-Release.com

- **Website Link – http://www.free-press-release.com**

Free-Press-Release.com is a press release distribution service, that since 2001 has helped small, medium and large sized enterprises optimize online marketing strategies. FPR is a matching service—bringing authors, publishers and social media together. Free-Press-Release.com's searchable database of hundreds of thousands of quality fresh articles is distributed to news engines, search engines and social bookmarking services immediately.

Craigslist.com

- **Website Link – http://www.craigslist.org**

Craigslist is a centralized network of online communities, featuring free online classified advertisements — with sections devoted to jobs, housing, personals, for sale, services, community, gigs, résumés, and discussion forums. Under community on the top left hand side is local news. This is a great free place to quickly post a press release.

Chapter 14
How to Remove Search Engine Information

Where to Begin – The Webmaster

Webmasters control websites, and website content. If you've found something on the Web that you'd like to have removed, your first effort should be to contact whoever controls that content. Most often, this means the webmaster of the page. You should ask them to take down the questionable content.

How to Contact a Webmaster

There are several ways to contact the webmaster:

- Find a 'Contact us' link or an email address for the webmaster on the site itself. This information is often easiest to find from the site's homepage.

- Look up a site's webmaster information using a special search called a 'Whois' ("who is?") search. You can perform a Whois search using Google: just search for [whois www.example.com] The result is sometimes a little messy, but you'll probably be able to find an email address.

- If you're unable to reach the webmaster, try contacting the site's hosting company, also usually listed in the Whois result.

And here's how to remove information from the following specific sites;

- Google
- Yahoo
- Blogger
- ZoomInfo.com

Removing Information from Google

To begin, sign in with your Google account to submit a removal request.

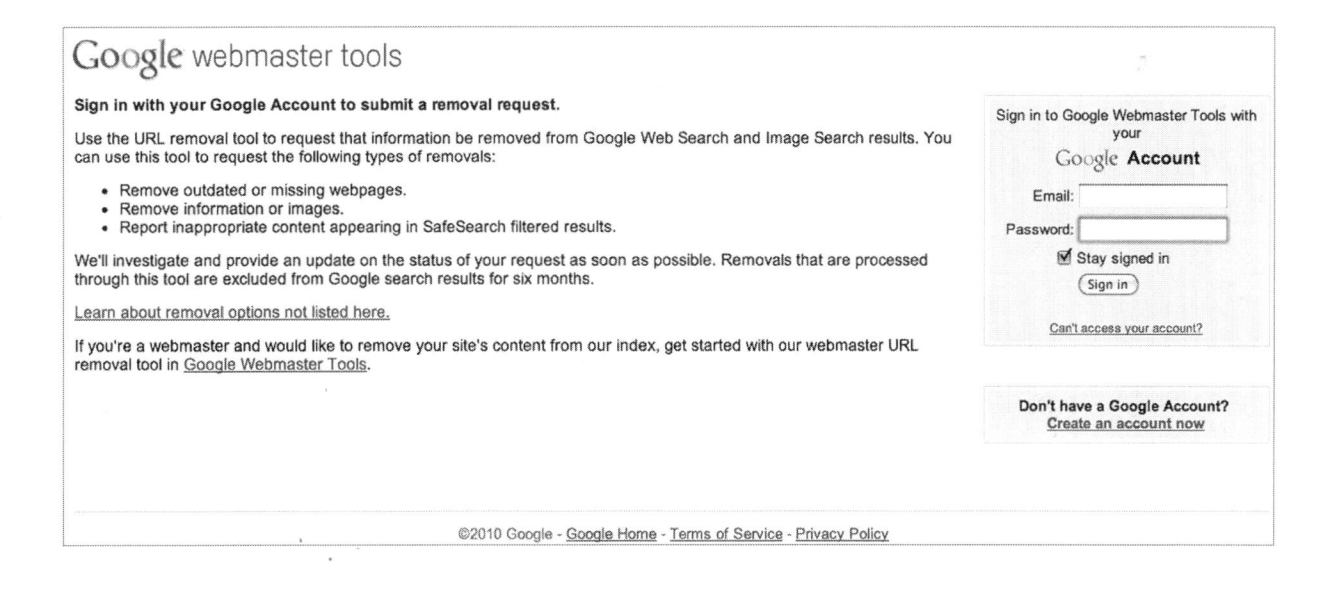

Google webmaster tools

Sign in with your Google Account to submit a removal request.

Use the URL removal tool to request that information be removed from Google Web Search and Image Search results. You can use this tool to request the following types of removals:

- Remove outdated or missing webpages.
- Remove information or images.
- Report inappropriate content appearing in SafeSearch filtered results.

We'll investigate and provide an update on the status of your request as soon as possible. Removals that are processed through this tool are excluded from Google search results for six months.

Learn about removal options not listed here.

If you're a webmaster and would like to remove your site's content from our index, get started with our webmaster URL removal tool in Google Webmaster Tools.

Sign in to Google Webmaster Tools with your Google **Account**

Email:
Password:
☑ Stay signed in
(Sign in)

Can't access your account?

Don't have a Google Account?
Create an account now

©2010 Google - Google Home - Terms of Service - Privacy Policy

Use the URL removal tool shown there to request that information be removed from Google Web Search and Image Search results. You can use this tool to request the following types of removals:

- Remove outdated or missing webpages.
- Remove information or images.
- Report inappropriate content appearing in SafeSearch filtered results.

Google will investigate and provide an update on the status of your request soon thereafter. Removals that are processed through this tool are excluded from Google search results for six months.

Once signed in Google will ask:

- What would you like removed?
- Do you need to remove sensitive information from Google?
- Is a dead link in our search results?

> **Google** **Webpage removal request tool**   myvois@gmail.com | My Account | Help | Sign out
>
> **My Removal Requests**
>
> Pending removal requests will be processed as soon as possible. Successful webpage removal requests will show a status of "Removed" and will be excluded from Google search results for 90 days. Successful SafeSearch removals will be excluded from Google SafeSearch results entirely. If your request is denied, click on the "Learn more" link for detailed information about why the removal was unsuccessful.
>
> (New Removal Request)   Show: ○ All ⦿ Pending only
>
> | Requested | URL | Removal Type | Status |
> |---|---|---|---|
> | | You have no pending removal requests. | | |
>
> If you're a webmaster and would like to remove your site's content from our index, get started with our webmaster URL removal tool in webmaster tools.
>
> © 2010 Google Inc. - Privacy

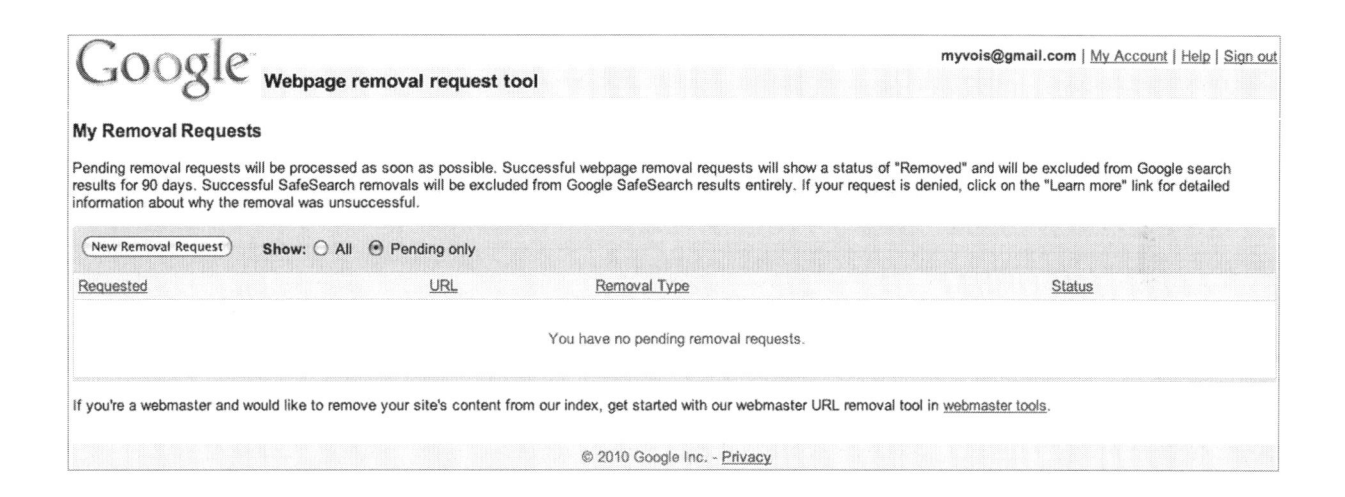

In a few limited cases, Google can provide additional assistance. But in most cases, the only way to change a search result is for the webmaster to change the site itself. However, Google is willing to help in a few cases including these:

- Social security or credit card information in results.

If you find a page in Google search results that lists your social security or credit card number, submit a webpage removal request. Google will contact the site's hosting company to request that the page be taken down from the Web. You don't want this information to be anywhere on the Web. So even if Google removes it from the search results, make sure to contact the webmaster directly and tell him or her to remove your information immediately.

And even if you have been unable to work with the site owner, Google will also remove the following as well if the information appearing in the search results is one of the following:

- Your social security or government ID number.
- Your bank account or credit card number.
- An image of your handwritten signature.
- Your full name or the name of your business appearing on an adult content site that's spamming Google's search results.

Removing Information from Yahoo

On this Yahoo page, you will find a summary of the required elements for an effective notification, and the Yahoo! contact information needed to submit those notifications. Yahoo! does enforce guidelines for search index inclusion or exclusion in order to protect the accuracy and correctness of search results. Yahoo says that websites or pages that are not in compliance with Search Content Quality Guidelines, or which contain objectionable content, may be removed from its index.

Yahoo! strives to provide the best search experience on the Web by directing high-quality and relevant web content in response to search queries, i.e.:

- Original and unique content of genuine value.
- Pages designed primarily for humans, with search engine considerations a secondary concern.

Yahoo! Search / AltaVista Report Abuse Form

* All fields required unless otherwise noted.

Please use this form only to report Yahoo! members who may be abusing our services or violating our terms of service. If you are looking for help with a Yahoo! service, please go to Yahoo! Help Central. There you will find an alphabetical list of all our services and products. To get help, click on the service that relates to the question or problem you have.

If you feel your intellectual property is being infringed and would like to file a notice, please view our Copyright/IP Policy.

What is your name and Yahoo! ID?
Name: (Optional)

Yahoo! ID: (Optional)
kjeffen

What is your email address?
Email Address:

Confirm Email Address

What is the violation?
Subject:

Enter additional information here:
Please tell us what you feel violates the Yahoo! Terms of Service. Please be as detailed and descriptive as you can. Where possible, be sure to identify specific content that is the subject of your report. Including web addresses (URLs) is also very helpful. The more you tell us about the circumstances you are reporting, the faster we will be able to investigate.

(Optional)

Submit

- Hyperlinks intended to help people find interesting, related content, when applicable.

- Metadata (including title and description) that accurately describes the contents of a web page.

- Good web design in general.

Unfortunately, not all web pages contain valuable information. Some pages are created deliberately to trick the search engine into offering inappropriate, redundant or poor-quality search results. This is often called "spam." Some, but not all, examples of the types of content that Yahoo! does not want include:

- Pages that harm the accuracy, diversity or relevance of search results.

- Pages dedicated to redirecting the user to another page (doorway pages).

- Multiple sites or pages offering substantially the same content.

- Sites with numerous, unnecessary virtual hostnames.
- Pages produced in great quantities, which have been automatically generated or which are of little value (cookie cutter pages).
- Pages using methods to artificially inflate search engine ranking. The use of text or links that are hidden from the user.
- Pages that give the search engine different content than what the end user sees (cloaking).
- Sites excessively cross linked with other sites to inflate a site's apparent popularity (link schemes).
- Pages built primarily for the search engines or pages with excessive or off-topic keywords.
- Misuse of competitor names.
- Multiple sites offering the same content.

- Sites that use excessive pop-ups which interfere with user navigation. Pages that seem deceptive, fraudulent, or provide a poor user experience.

Yahoo! says that its search content quality guidelines "are designed to ensure that poor-quality pages do not degrade the user experience in any way. As with other Yahoo! guidelines, Yahoo! reserves the right, at its sole discretion, to take any and all action it deems appropriate to ensure the quality of its search index."

Removing Information From Blogger

Blogger takes violations of its Terms of Service very seriously. After careful review, Blogger says it may remove content or place a content warning page before viewing content deemed offensive, harmful, or dangerous, such as:

- Hate against a protected group
- Adult or pornographic images

- Promotion of dangerous and illegal activity
- Content facilitating phishing or account hijacking
- Impersonated user identity

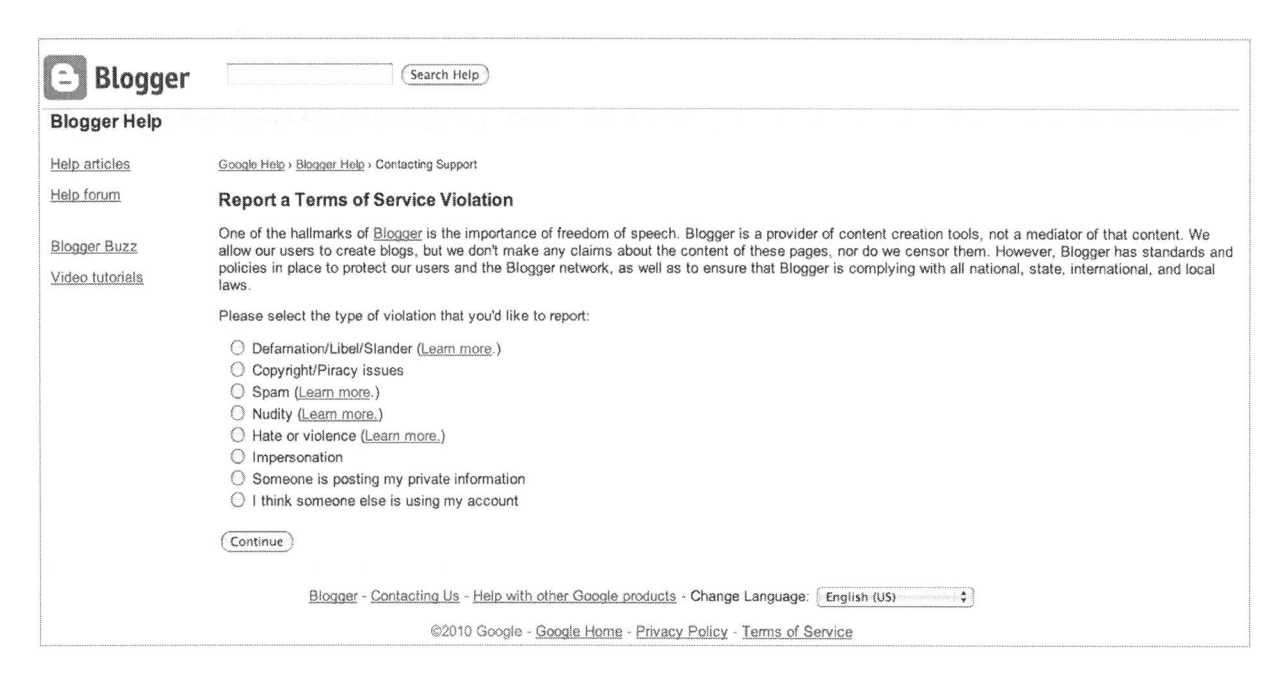

Blogger

Blogger Help

Help articles
Help forum
Blogger Buzz
Video tutorials

Google Help › Blogger Help › Contacting Support

Report a Terms of Service Violation

One of the hallmarks of Blogger is the importance of freedom of speech. Blogger is a provider of content creation tools, not a mediator of that content. We allow our users to create blogs, but we don't make any claims about the content of these pages, nor do we censor them. However, Blogger has standards and policies in place to protect our users and the Blogger network, as well as to ensure that Blogger is complying with all national, state, international, and local laws.

Please select the type of violation that you'd like to report:

○ Defamation/Libel/Slander (Learn more.)
○ Copyright/Piracy issues
○ Spam (Learn more.)
○ Nudity (Learn more.)
○ Hate or violence (Learn more.)
○ Impersonation
○ Someone is posting my private information
○ I think someone else is using my account

(Continue)

Blogger - Contacting Us - Help with other Google products - Change Language: [English (US)]

©2010 Google - Google Home - Privacy Policy - Terms of Service

Unfortunately, Blogger is a provider of content creation tools, not a mediator of content. As such, it allows users users to create blogs, but doesn't make any claims about the content of those pages. To the point, here are some examples of content Blogger will not remove unless ordered to do so by a court order:

- Personal attacks or alleged defamation
- Parody or satire of individuals
- Distasteful imagery or language
- Political or social commentary

Removing Information At ZoomInfo

The people at ZoomInfo are pretty cooperative when it comes to removing information from a profile, compiled and based on other Internet sources it crawls. To have something removed simply search for your profile at http://www.zoominfo.com/ and then claim it. Claiming your profile is essentially the same as joining. Once you have claimed your profile simply send remove@zoominfo.com an email stating the following:

"Hello ZoomInfo Product Support; As a ZoomInfo member I would like to make a request. There is an online source that has written some untrue things about me. The online source I am referring to is listed on my profile page and I would like it if you could remove it from your list of online sources. I appreciate your help please see the online sourced material to be removed below. Thank you in advance."

First Response

You will immediately receive a form letter like the one below from ZoomInfo Product Support:

"Thank you for contacting ZoomInfo. A copy of your message appears below. You can expect to receive a response from us within one business day. To help track your inquiry we have generated a reference number. Your ticket code is XXXXXXXXXXXX. Please use this code in any further communication — Zoom Information Inc. www.zoominfo.com.

If the problem isn't fixed within a day, reply to ZoomInfo Product Support at WebSupport@zoominfo.com and simply ask for an update as follows:

"ZoomInfo Product Support I am following up on an email I sent to you a few days ago. My ticket code is XXXXXXXXXXX, Could you please give me an update. Thank you."

Follow-Up

The next letter you will receive will be as follows.

"Thank you for writing to ZoomInfo. ZoomInfo is a specialized web search engine, similar to Google but focused on finding information about companies and professionals. All of ZoomInfo's information comes from corporate websites, press releases, SEC filings, and other public websites.

"ZoomInfo mostly contains information about business professionals found in these sources, including title, company name and work experience. We will add the noted web source on your profile to the queue for removal and send you a confirmation via email when the process is complete. The removal should take 24-48 hours. Please let me know if you have any additional questions. Product Support Zoom Information, Inc."

"In case this email does not fully answer your question, or you would like to contact us for any reason, simply reply to this email. Reference number: XXXXXXXXXX. Please use this ticket number in any correspondence with us. Thank you for writing to ZoomInfo."

After Removal

After honoring your request, you'll receive this letter:

"At your request, the noted web source on your web profile has been removed from ZoomInfo. We apologize for any inconvenience. ZoomInfo is a specialized web search engine, similar to Google but focused on finding information about companies and professionals. The information found in ZoomInfo's search results comes from corporate websites, press releases, SEC filings, and other public websites.

"Please be aware that new information about you may appear on the Internet at some point in the future. If you are active in any public arenas (board memberships, news interviews, community groups, conferences, seminars, professional organizations, and so on) there is a high probability that these organizations will publish new information about you on their websites.

"In turn, ZoomInfo may read this new data and construct an independent profile unconnected to the one you have asked to be removed. ZoomInfo will exercise best efforts to prevent such information from appearing in our search results, but due to the automated nature of the process we cannot guarantee that information about you on these independent profiles will fail to appear in our search results.

"Also, keep in mind that references to a removed web profile may continue to appear in external search engines such as Google or Yahoo until those companies index the ZoomInfo site and learn that the web profile no longer exists. ZoomInfo can do nothing to speed up this process. Please let me know if you have any additional questions.   Product Support Zoom Information, Inc"

Chapter 15
Online Reputation Management is Ongoing

Today – Tomorrow – Forever

You did it. You have done all you can do and now you are satisfied with your Online Reputation - time to sit back right?

Not unless you want to have all of your efforts wasted.

Remember, just about anyone can put themselves in a position to be involved in forming your reputation, so you need to continue to stay aware what is being said about you online.

As demonstrated in this book, things change instantly online. Doing a Google search on your name last week and finding everything OK is fine.

But that was last week.

This week things could change rapidly and dramatically.

Keep following the alerts you set up. Monitor online chatter. Your reputation will constantly be challenged by other people.

Negative news tends to travel fast and far on the web. It's incredibly easy for someone to post something negative on a blog, which can then get picked up and shared on Facebook, or Twitter, where it can then be picked up by search engines.

You have done the hard work. Now simply monitoring your reputation will make it much easier to continue to combat the negative before it gets out of control.

Made in the USA
San Bernardino, CA
09 November 2012